D1591109

Hiking Trails
in the Collegiate Peaks
Wilderness Area

Hiking Trails in the Collegiate Peaks Wilderness Area

Lora Davis

with photographs and maps by the author

PRUETT PUBLISHING COMPANY
BOULDER, COLORADO

© 1994 by Lora Davis

ALL RIGHTS RESERVED. No part of this book may be reproduced without written permission from the publisher, except in the case of brief excerpts in critical reviews and articles. Address all inquiries to: Pruett Publishing Company, 2928 Pearl Street, Boulder, Colorado 80301.

Printed in the United States

10 9 8 7 6 5 4 3 2 1

Library of Congress Cataloging-in-Publication Data

Davis, Lora, 1946-
    Hiking trails in the Collegiate Peaks Wilderness Area / Lora
Davis, with photographs and maps by the author.
        p.   cm.
    Includes bibliographical references and index.
    ISBN 0-87108-847-9 (pbk. : alk. paper)
    1. Hiking—Colorado—Collegiate Peaks Wilderness Area—Guidebooks.
    2. Trails—Colorado—Collegiate Peaks Wilderness Area—Guidebooks.
    3. Collegiate Peaks Wilderness Area (Colo.)—Guidebooks. I. Title.
    GV199.42.C62C643   1994
    796.5' 1' 097884—dc20   94-2898
                                                                CIP

Holy Earth Mother, the trees and all nature are witnesses of your thoughts and deeds.

—Winnebago tribe

The Collegiate Peaks Wilderness Area exists because of the ongoing work and financial support of many dedicated individuals and organizations. In consideration of this, a percentage of the author's royalties will be donated to local nonprofit environmental groups dedicated to the continuing preservation of wilderness and all that it encompasses.

To my grandchildren,
Catherine and David,
and their grandchildren,
and their grandchildren's grandchildren.
May I live my life in such a way
that the wilderness will be preserved
for them to experience.

Contents

Introduction

The Collegiate Peaks Wilderness Area offers itself to all types of mountain enthusiasts—hikers, backpackers, fishermen, hunters, modern gold prospectors, photographers, out-of-state visitors—the list is as varied as the people who visit the area. All enjoy the opportunity to be in and experience wilderness in their own unique ways.

Several campgrounds dot the borders of the Collegiate Peaks Wilderness, making it accessible to families with young children and to visitors from out of state. You'll often find the campgrounds full, and numerous people penetrate the area's boundaries in the peak of the summer. Once within the boundaries of Wilderness you must go on foot, but many of the four-wheel-drive roads surrounding the area lend themselves well to mountain biking in the summer and cross-country skiing in the winter.

The Wilderness Area drapes across the Continental Divide from Cottonwood Pass on the south border and reaches almost to Independence Pass on the north. Hiking trails often follow old mining or logging roads, which themselves probably follow some of the routes the Utes used as they moved from mountains to plains with the seasons. The scarcity of trails in the northwestern end of the area is an indication of the ruggedness and solitude found there. The southeastern half, more accessible to the densely populated areas of the Front Range, has a greater number of trails, some extending from one side of the Divide to the other.

The trails become fainter and the crowds sparse as you enter just a few miles into the depths of the Wilderness Area. Here is the real beauty of wilderness—high alpine lakes and the music of waterfalls; the sheer rock faces of the peaks along the Continental Divide; a passing deer, tipping her head to the side in a gesture of curious interest; a bear meandering past across the valley, making your heart miss a beat; solitude and immense silence; brilliant starry skies and a full moon that unexpectedly pops over a ridge, taking your breath away. Only the most hard-hearted could come here, spend a night or two, and leave unchanged.

The purpose of this guide is to introduce you to the area. Any of the trails described can be hiked fully or partially in a day. The area lends itself particularly well to backpacking—my own favorite way to explore the Wilderness. Trails interconnect and cross the Divide, allowing you to begin an extended hike near Buena Vista and end near Aspen, or cross from Taylor Park to Independence Pass Road.

1

This is not meant to be a definitive guide to the Collegiate Peaks Wilderness. Rather, it is an introduction. If one were to spend an entire lifetime there, it's doubtful that the full extent of the area within the boundaries could be explored. I have focused primarily on existing trails. Most are in good condition, some follow old mining roads, a few are so faint as to be almost nonexistent at times. My hope is that you'll use this guide as a starting point to explore, and that you will come to love this area as much as I have.

What is Wilderness?

"Where the imprint of humans is substantially unnoticeable."

The idea of protecting wilderness arose in the early 1900s. At that time, the conservationist Aldo Leopold proposed a new management plan for public lands. Under this plan, logging would be restricted to the most accessible forests and the remainder would be reserved for recreation, game protection, and wilderness. In 1924, under his guidance, a 500,000-acre area in the Gila National Forest became the first federal land designated as wilderness. At about the same time, Arthur Carhart, a landscape architect for the U.S. Forest Service, fought to establish the Superior Primitive Area, now known as the Boundary Waters Canoe Area.

The procedures for designating a wilderness area were finally formulated in 1929. In 1964 the United States government established, through legislation, a formal recognition of wilderness. The Wilderness Act, adopted that year, set up the Wilderness Preservation System. This conservation legislation established for the American people an enduring resource of wilderness. The act defines wilderness in part as areas that:

1) provide outstanding opportunities for solitude and a primitive unconfined type of recreation.
2) may contain ecological, geological, or other features of scenic, scientific, or historical value.
3) are affected primarily by the forces of nature, where the imprints of humans is substantially unnoticeable.
4) are undeveloped and federally protected and managed so as to allow natural processes to continue.
5) are formally designated by Congress as wilderness.

Steadily increasing use and other human influences are affecting wilderness qualities. The preservation of these qualities can best be insured through careful management and public understanding and support.

The Collegiate Peaks Wilderness Area

The Collegiate Peaks Wilderness Area, created on December 22, 1980, encompasses nearly 168,000 acres. Its southernmost point reaches almost to Buena Vista. From here it extends west toward Taylor Park along Cottonwood Pass Road, and north toward Leadville along U.S.

3

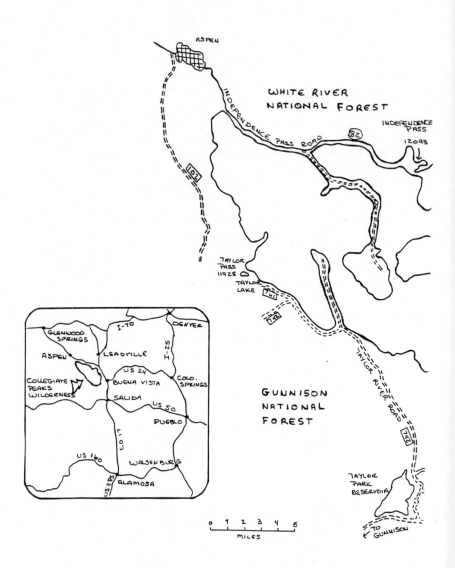

The Collegiate Peaks Wilderness Area

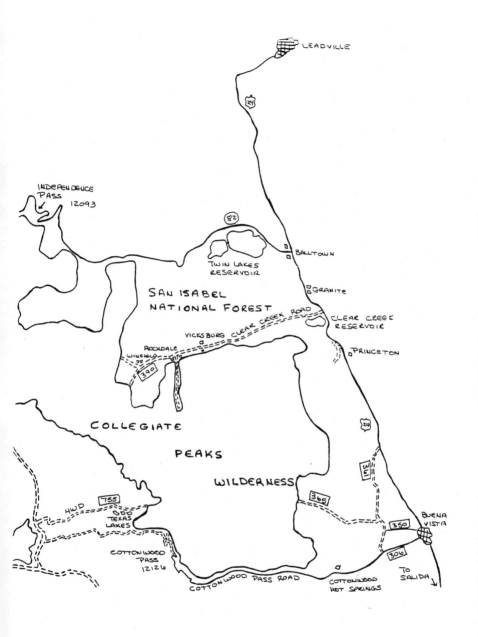

LEADVILLE

24

INDEPENDENCE
PASS   12093

82

BALLTOWN

TWIN LAKES
RESERVOIR

GRANITE

SAN ISABEL
NATIONAL FOREST

CLEAR CREEK ROAD

VICKSBURG

CLEAR CREEK
RESERVOIR

ROCKDALE

PRINCETON

WINFIELD
390

390

COLLEGIATE

PEAKS

24

WILDERNESS

398

4WD   755

365

ODO
TEXAS
LAKES

350

BUENA
VISTA

COTTONWOOD
PASS
12126

306

TO
SALIDA

COTTONWOOD PASS ROAD

COTTONWOOD
HOT SPRINGS

Highway 24. Bounded on the north by Independence Pass Road, it stretches northwest toward Aspen. It resides within the boundaries of three national forests—the White River, the Gunnison, and the San Isabel. Elevations range from 9,500 feet to over 14,000 feet. Contained within its boundaries are eight of the highest peaks in the state. Numerous other peaks, though under 14,000 feet, offer high challenge to even the strongest local mountaineers. Many of the area's peaks, even those over 14,000 feet, can be scaled by anyone in reasonably good physical condition. All that is needed are good basic hiking equipment, an understanding of map and compass use, and adequate knowledge of mountain weather and safety. Interestingly, some of the most challenging peaks in the area are under 14,000 feet.

The area was named for a section of the Sawatch Range known as the Collegiate Peaks. Sawatch—originally the Ute word *Saguache*—means "waters of the blue earth." From the town of Buena Vista to the east, the Collegiate Peaks dominate the view. J. D. Whitney, for whom California's Mount Whitney is designated, named the individual peaks after colleges. He was head of the first graduating class of the Harvard School of Mining and christened the highest peak in the range Mount Harvard. The second highest was named Mount Yale, after his own alma mater. Mount Princeton (which lies outside the Wilderness boundary), Mount Columbia, and Mount Oxford were named later, in keeping with the theme. Missouri Mountain, Mount Belford, La Plata Peak, and Huron Peak complete the list of peaks over 14,000 feet within the boundaries of the Wilderness Area.

Though little information is available, it is probable that the Mountain Ute roamed throughout this area prior to possession of the land by early white settlers. No one knows for sure where the Utes came from originally. They were living throughout the mountains of Colorado and Utah when other tribes arrived, and their legends state that they were created in these mountains by the Great Spirit. They sometimes hunted buffalo on the plains but always returned to the mountains as their home. The verdant valleys, fish-filled streams, and occasional hot springs throughout this area no doubt offered a bountiful life to the many groups of people who traveled from the open plains of the eastern slope to the lush farm and grazing lands on the western slope of the Divide.

As gold and silver fever spread among the white settlers, the Utes were forcibly removed from the area. Dozens of mining towns and camps sprang up—wild towns filled with dance halls and bars—Everett, Vicksburg, Winfield, Hangmans Camp, to name just a few. Many of these towns thrived for only a few years, and often the only remaining signs of their existence are mine tailings and the scars left by overlogging. The buildings of the towns and camps have long since fallen to the ground or been carried away by the thousands of tourists, hikers, and souvenir seekers passing through here over the years. Today only a relatively few remain.

Wilderness Use

The continuing preservation of this and other wilderness areas requires that certain recommendations and regulations be followed. Mechanized transportation such as automobiles, mountain bicycles, motorcycles, hang gliders, all-terrain vehicles, and snowmobiles are prohibited within the boundaries. Use of power saws or other motorized equipment is also not allowed. Because of their impact on wildlife, it is recommended that dogs not be taken into the Wilderness Area. If you do, the dog must at all times be kept on a leash no longer than six feet. The maximum size of groups is twenty-five people and/or pack or saddle stock (twenty-five "heartbeats"). It is recommended that you follow minimum-impact camping policies:

Food Storage and Disposal. Pack out all garbage. Store food and garbage in a stuff sack and suspend it from a tree ten feet from the ground and four feet out from the tree.

Fires. Please use a gas stove for cooking as an alternative to campfires. If you do have a campfire, keep it small and limit its use to late evening and early morning. Collect only dead and downed wood no larger around than the size of your wrist—even downed timber is an important component of the ecosystem. Establish fires no closer than one hundred feet from streams, and use only an existing fire ring. Attend fires at all times.

Campsite. Camp no less than one hundred feet from streams, lakes, and trails. When possible, share tents. If camping with a large group, limit the number of tents at each site to two or three.

Water Use. Use only biodegradable soaps or, preferably, no soap. Do all washing at least 150 feet from water sources.

Human Waste. Bury human waste in shallow holes six to eight inches deep and two hundred feet away from water sources or trails. Build a latrine if camping for more than a few nights with several people. Always pack out your toilet tissue.

By following the few simple regulations as well as the additional low-impact camping and hiking policies, we can preserve wilderness areas for generations to come.

I have observed in my own life and in the lives of others that there is also change in everyday living habits as a result of spending time in and becoming conscious of our impact on the wilderness. I cherish *all* of the environment more, not just the wilderness. Too often our impact on our surroundings goes unnoticed. Trash is whisked away from the front yard once a week, chemicals are washed down the drain and "disappear," lawn fertilizers and pesticides *seem* to improve the immediate surroundings. Partly through my hiking and backpacking experiences, I have become more conscious of the delicacy and beauty of the world and my impact on it. I use less or biodegradable household chemicals, I walk and carpool more, and I am more conscious of resource use, reuse, and recycling. This is after all our home, and a very nice one at that.

Using This Guide

Maps

A hand-drawn map of the Collegiate Peaks Wilderness Area is presented on pages 4 and 5. This map has been divided into several smaller sections that contain from one to five hikes each. An attempt has been made to limit the number of trailheads in each of the section maps and to have the hikes begin from the same road. This goal was not always achieved, due to the unusual shape of the Collegiate Peaks Wilderness Area. The maps in this guide are *not* intended to be used as hiking aids but simply to define and locate general areas.

It is recommended that you never hike in a wilderness area without the aid of a topographic map, a compass, and a solid understanding of the use of each. The Forest Service, along with the help of hundreds of volunteers each year, does a tremendous job of maintaining the trail systems. However, to enter the Collegiate Peaks Wilderness on the assumption that the trail will appear exactly as described or as shown on a map is foolhardy. Weather, animals, and lack of use or overuse by humans can all but erase portions of a trail at times. In high-use areas, the Forest Service often changes the course of a trail to allow for revegetation.

Three different types of maps are recommended: U.S. Forest Service maps, U.S. Geological Survey topographic maps (referred to as "quads" or 7½-minute), and Trails Illustrated topographic maps. Each type of map provides different information. All three types are not necessarily required to enjoy most areas.

The U.S. Forest Service maps are best used to define the general area. They indicate roads, trails, and water supplies, as well as nearby campgrounds. However, altitude and terrain are not shown on these maps, hence it is not recommended that they be used as hiking guides. Always check the date these maps were last updated. Man-made landmarks such as roads and fences tend to change faster than maps do. I often use Forest Service maps to get to the trailhead and perhaps locate a good initial campsite or campground.

The USGS topographic maps are high-detail terrain maps. They cover approximately fifty square miles and indicate terrain, vegetation, and water supplies, as well as man-made landmarks such as roads, buildings, mines, and fences. They are essential for hiking in a wilderness area, especially if you plan to stray from a high-use area. Even in a high-use area, though, where trails are well maintained and well marked, people often stray off the trail, creating new "trails" and confusion for future hikers.

The Trails Illustrated maps are topographic maps also but cover an area several times that covered by the USGS maps. Though they are expensive, only four Trails Illustrated maps are required to cover the entire Collegiate Peaks Wilderness Area. These maps give a broader view of the area and so are excellent aids to extended backpacking trips. They are made of high-quality waterproof paper, a feature you will come to love if you hike in the thunderstorm-prone mountains of Colorado for long. I use both the USGS 7½-minute topographic map and the Trails Illustrated map when I am hiking. The USGS maps have more detail, while the Trails Illustrated maps cover a larger area. This gives a better perspective of the area, and comparing them can be a great help when the route is not clear.

The following maps cover the entire Collegiate Peaks region:

U.S. Geological Survey Maps (USGS Quads; 7½-minute): Aspen, Buena Vista West, Granite, Harvard Lakes, Hayden Peak, Independence Pass, Italian Creek, Mount Elbert, Mount Harvard, Mount Yale, New York Peak, Pieplant, Taylor Park Reservoir, Tincup, and Winfield.

Trails Illustrated Maps: Collegiate Peaks, Independence Pass, Leadville/Fairplay, and Crested Butte/Pearl Pass.

U.S. Forest Service Maps (USFS): Gunnison National Forest, San Isabel National Forest, and White River National Forest.

Destination

In most cases, the destination is a scenic site such as a lake, a pass, or a peak summit. Occasionally the described trail connects to other trails and the "destination" is not easily defined. When this is the case, the destination becomes quite subjective. In these instances an attempt is made to indicate connections with the other trails. These trails are usually defined under the "recommended use" category as extended backpacking trails (such as the multiple trails in the Texas Creek area). Follow your own initiative and interest to define for yourself how best to use the descriptions presented here.

Distance, Elevation, and Elevation Gain

The distance is given as either round-trip or one-way distance from the point at which you begin hiking. Generally, if the trail is a connecting trail, the one-way distance between the connecting trails is given. If there is a well-defined destination, the round-trip distance is given. Unless otherwise stated, all the trailheads are accessible by two-wheel-drive passenger cars, though the roads may at times be rough, for example in the early summer following spring runoff. The trail description, distance, and elevation gain is always given from the point at which a standard automobile can no longer be driven. If you own a four-wheel-drive vehicle, you may at times be able to drive a portion of the way, thereby shortening your hike or allowing you to "car camp" away from the main road. It is my preference to walk and backpack as much as possible, though I occasionally drive to the Wilderness boundary. I realize that not everyone is interested in or capable of backpacking—for example, young children or people with injuries. However, I encourage those who are able to pursue the possibility. Aside from the fact that our feet and breath create significantly less environmental damage than an auto's wheels and exhaust, opportunities to drive abound in our fast-paced society, while opportunities to walk and enjoy our surroundings seem to be more limited.

The starting elevation is the elevation at the trailhead, or in the case of a connecting trail, the elevation at the trail intersections. Generally, the maximum elevation is attained at the destination, but occasionally you will cross a saddle or pass and drop back down to a valley or lake. The elevation gain given is the total elevation gained over the hike. For example, if the trailhead is at 9,000 feet, the destination is a lake at 10,000 feet, and you cross a 12,000-foot pass to reach the lake, then the elevation gain is 5,000 feet (3,000 feet of elevation gained on the way in and 2,000 feet gained on the return trip when you climb the pass again). If the destination lake were at the high point of 12,000 feet, the elevation gain would be 3,000 feet.

Rating

The hike classifications are made in terms of walking distances, elevation gain, and difficulty levels of the various routes. As previously defined, elevation gain is the total elevation gained over the hike. Generally, this corresponds closely to the difference between the beginning elevation and the ending elevation. However, on moderate or difficult hikes more than one high point is occasionally attained, or one may have to cross a high pass to reach the final destination. In this event, the additional elevation is added to obtain the total gain. Considerations such as the presence or absence of a trail, the presence of scree or talus, the necessity of bouldering, and the degree of bushwhacking necessary are also included in the determination of the classification. The following rules are general only. A trail that is easy based solely on mileage and elevation gain may be quite difficult if one must rely on map and compass to find a route.

As a general rule, an easy hike has a maximum distance of eight miles round trip with an elevation gain less than 2,000 feet. The entire trip is on good trail. An adult or child in average good health could be expected to complete an easy hike with little or no difficulty.

A moderate hike involves a maximum distance up to twelve miles and a total elevation gain of no more than 2,500 feet. There may be some off-trail hiking. Hikers should be in moderately good physical condition with adequate hiking experience and an awareness of some basic survival skills.

A difficult hike covers a round-trip distance of more than twelve miles with an elevation gain over 2,500 feet. Scree, steep grass, rock, route-finding, or other rough terrain problems may be encountered. Hikers should be in excellent physical condition and prepared to spend the night, if necessary.

Occasionally a hike may be classified as difficult based solely on its distance. These cases are noted, and it is up to the individual whether to attempt the entire hike in a day, to complete a portion before returning, or to treat the hike as an overnight trip. In determining classification, no consideration is made whether the trip is a day hike or a backpack.

Time Allowed

The time allowed for each hike is a function both of the elevation gain and the distance. The basic standard used is two miles and 500 feet of elevation gain per hour when hiking with just a daypack. Additional time is allowed for such factors as increased steepness, off-trail hiking, and high elevation. For example, a four-mile hike on good trail beginning at 9,000 feet with an elevation gain of 1,000 feet would normally take two hours. This same hike begun at 11,000 feet and over rough terrain might take four hours. Increase the time allowed by at least fifty percent if you plan to backpack.

Recommended Use

Hikes are recommended as day hike, overnight backpack, or extended backpack. A day hike is one that can be completed in a day and may lack suitable campsites. A lack of campsites may be due to any one of a number of conditions—heavy use of the area, high altitude and delicate tundra, or steeply sloping terrain, to name just a few. Any of the hikes in this guide may be hiked partway and treated as a day hike. You need not necessarily reach the final, defined destination to enjoy the hike. A trip classified as an overnight backpack for which you carry overnight camping equipment means that because of the length, scenic attractions, possible side and loop trips, or the availability of good campsites, you may prefer to take two or more days to complete it. Extended backpack trips are those that are too long to make in one day, assuming one hikes the entire distance, or that may connect to other trails and require a car shuttle if the beginning and ending trailheads are not the same.

This is not meant to be a definitive guide to the Collegiate Peaks Wilderness Area. There are enough mining roads, trails, lakes, high meadows, passes, and peaks here to last one a lifetime. If you were to hike all the trails in this guide you would have a solid knowledge of this area. From that, you could begin more advanced hikes and backpacks. We are fortunate in Colorado to have an extensive wilderness system. Increasing population *will* impact it, no doubt. But if we, as our Native American ancestors did, try to think seven generations ahead, there is hope that there will always be enough wildness in this world to meet the needs of all our relations.

Beyond the wall of the unreal city, beyond the security fences topped with barbed wire and razor wire, beyond the asphalt beltings of the super-highways, beyond the cemented banksides of our temporarily stopped and mutilated rivers, beyond the lies that poison the air, there is another world waiting for you. It is the old true world of the deserts, the mountains, the forests, the islands, the shores, the open plains. Go there. Be there. Walk gently and quietly deep within it. And then—May your trails be dim, lonesome, stony, narrow, winding and only slightly uphill. May the wind bring rain for the slickrock potholes fourteen miles on the other side of yonder blue ridge. May God's dog serenade your campfire, may the rattlesnake and the screech owl amuse your reverie, may the Great Sun dazzle your eyes by day and the Great Bear watch over you by night.
Edward Abbey
Beyond the Wall

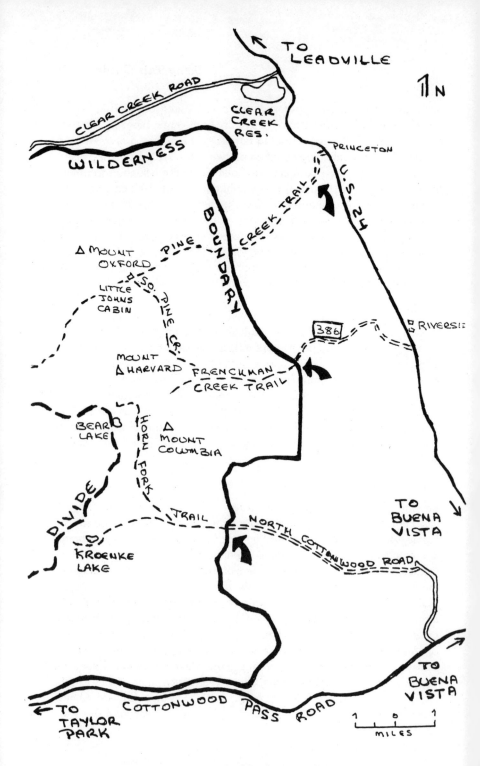

Collegiate Peaks Wilderness Area—Eastern Portion

Hikes in the Eastern Area

The hikes in this area are all approached from the thirty-five-mile stretch of U.S. Highway 24 between Leadville and Buena Vista. A number of short day hikes, access to the Colorado Trail, access to several of the area's 14,000-foot peaks, and access to routes over the Continental Divide for extended backpacking trips all combine to make this one of the most popular regions in the Collegiate Peaks Wilderness. The trailheads may be crowded in midsummer, and the trails are generally well marked and well maintained. On a weekend in the peak of the summer you're almost guaranteed to find other hikers here. Many of the trails are surrounded by aspen at the lower elevations, making early fall a beautiful time to enjoy this area.

Horn Fork Trail #1449

Destination: *Bear Lake*
Round-trip distance: *11 miles*
Starting elevation: *9,880 feet*
Maximum elevation: *12,370 feet*
Elevation gain: *2,490 feet*
Rating: *Difficult*
Time allowed: *12 hours*
Recommended use: *Day hike or overnight backpack. Good all-around hiking area. Access to Mount Columbia and Mount Harvard.*
Maps: *San Isabel National Forest; 7½' Mount Yale; 7½' Mount Harvard; Trails Illustrated Collegiate Peaks*

Trailhead Access

From the light at the intersection of U.S. Highway 24 and County Road 306 in Buena Vista, drive two and one-half miles west on paved CR306 to CR361. Turn right (north) and drive approximately two miles to CR365. Turn left (west) and follow this good gravel road approximately two and one-half miles to the boundary of the San Isabel National Forest.

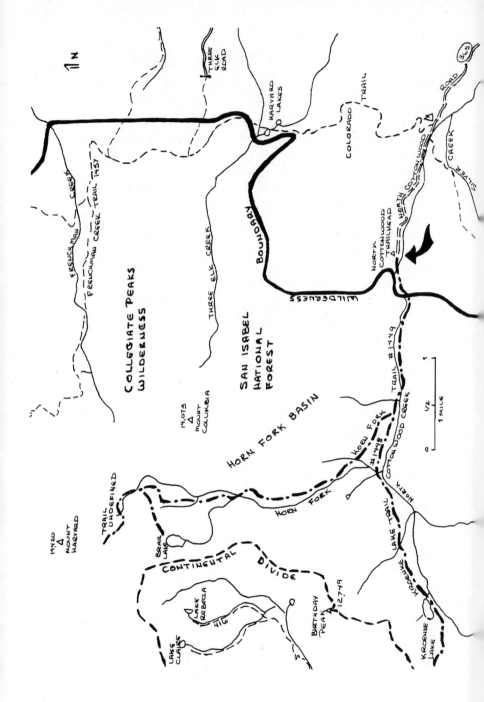

Horn Fork Trail #1449, Kroenke Lake Trail #1448

The road becomes increasingly rough but is still easily accessible by a two-wheel-drive automobile. Continue on another three miles, crossing the Colorado Trail twice. The North Cottonwood trailhead provides ample parking, though it is crowded at times because it provides access to a fairly large area. The trailhead access is the same as for Kroenke Lake Trail #1448 (see page 20).

Trail Description

From the North Cottonwood trailhead you have access to Horn Fork Basin, from which you may climb two 14,000-foot peaks. At the north end of the basin is Mount Harvard, the third highest point in Colorado at 14,420 feet. Mount Columbia stands sentinel to the east and is the thirty-fifth highest peak at 14,073 feet. If you enjoy the solitude of an alpine lake, you may wish to spend some time at high-altitude Bear Lake. The Horn Fork Basin provides the opportunity for a day hike or a strenuous peak ascent, a weekend backpack or the starting point for a long stay in one of the most beautiful Wilderness Areas in Colorado.

The hike begins at the well-marked trailhead at the west end of the parking area. The trail to Horn Fork Basin heads west on the north side of North Cottonwood Creek, then crosses to the south side within one-quarter mile. At one-half mile (10,200 feet) you enter the Collegiate Peaks Wilderness Area. It feels almost like a rainforest along this portion of the trail—dense fir, aspen, and lodgepole pine surround you, with lupine and fern for ground cover. Though you can no longer see North Cottonwood Creek, its gentle music accompanies you along the trail.

At approximately one and one-quarter miles, the trail passes through an old avalanche chute and crosses a bridge to the north side of North Cottonwood Creek. Before crossing, look to the south-southwest. The east ridge of Mount Yale (14,196 feet) is just visible behind the top of the avalanche chute. One of the easier peaks (for climbing) over 14,000 feet, it is usually approached from the Browns Pass Trail west of the peak.

At slightly less than two miles, you reach the Forest Service sign directing you to either Kroenke Lake or Bear Lake. Take the right fork (to Bear Lake). The trail now begins a short traverse and a series of switchbacks up a steep slope. This steep section lasts less than one-quarter mile before the trail levels out again and begins a steady, gentle climb. There are a number of beautiful campsites through this area for those wishing to spend a day or two climbing and exploring. As the altitude increases, the forest becomes a little less dense. At about three and one-half miles,

At an altitude of 12,400 feet, pristine Bear Lake is still frozen in mid-July.

Mount Columbia breaks majestically into view to the northeast. The trail again begins to climb for a short distance before finally leaving the forest and rising above timberline. The route continues on for another mile, rising gently and winding through the willows above Horn Fork Creek. There is one more short, steep ascent at the end of the basin before the path curves to the west and the final short walk to Bear Lake. This alpine lake high above timberline is surrounded by rock and fragile tundra and may remain partially frozen throughout the summer. Because of the delicacy of this ecosystem, it is advisable to camp lower in the valley, near the willows, if you wish to spend the night in the basin.

If you are interested in climbing Mount Harvard (14,420 feet), continue north from the trail at the end of the basin, just before it turns west for the final approach to Bear Lake. The trail is undefined but is marked by cairn for the turning point. Follow the terrain and make the final approach from the southwest shoulder. A relatively easy climb among the 14,000-foot peaks, this is still long and strenuous if attempted in one day. The overall elevation gain from trailhead to summit is 4,540 feet, and the round-trip distance is almost thirteen miles.

14,420-foot Mount Harvard, in the center of this photo, stands at the north end of Horn Fork Basin.

To climb 14,073-foot Mount Columbia, follow Mount Harvard's gentle shoulder southeast for one-half mile. From here, drop down 1,600 feet into the Frenchman Creek Basin to the north of Mount Columbia. Head almost directly south, avoiding the loose rock and cliffs, to gain Columbia's east ridge for the final approach. To return to camp in the Horn Fork Basin, follow any one of a number of steep scree slopes down the western side of Mount Columbia. An easier approach begins and ends in the Frenchman Creek Basin, which is reached via Frenchman Creek Trail #1457 (see page 23).

If a man walk in the woods for love of them half of each day, he is in danger of being regarded as a loafer; but if he spends his whole day as a speculator, shearing off those woods and making earth bald before her time, he is esteemed an industrious and enterprising citizen. As if a town had no interest in its forest but to cut them down!

Henry David Thoreau

Kroenke Lake Trail #1448

(Refer to map on page 16.)

Destination: *Kroenke Lake*
Round-trip distance: *8 miles*
Starting elevation: *9,880 feet*
Maximum elevation: *11,520 feet*
Elevation gain: *1,640 feet*
Rating: *Easy*
Time allowed: *7 hours*
Recommended use: *Day hike, overnight, or extended backpack. Popular destination for fishermen, day hikers, and weekend backpackers. Trail continues on to Brown's Pass Trail for extended hikes.*
Maps: *San Isabel National Forest; 7½' Mount Yale; 7½' Mount Harvard; Trails Illustrated Collegiate Peaks*

Trailhead Access

From the light at the intersection of U.S. Highway 24 and County Road 306 in Buena Vista, drive two and one-half miles west on paved CR306 to CR361. Turn right (north) and drive approximately two miles to CR365. Turn left (west) and follow this good gravel road two and one-half miles to the boundary of the San Isabel National Forest. The road becomes increasingly rough but is still easily accessible by two-wheel-drive. Continue on another three miles, crossing the Colorado Trail twice. The North Cottonwood trailhead provides ample parking, though it is at times quite crowded because this trailhead is used to reach a fairly large area. The trailhead access is the same as for Horn Fork Trail #1449 (page 15).

Trail Description

This trail appeals to a wide range of wilderness enthusiasts. Kroenke Lake is a popular destination for fishermen, day hikers, and weekend backpackers. A small island sits in the middle of the lake, providing a final challenge to those who always desire to reach the most inaccessible

A small island in the center of Kroenke Lake offers a final challenge to hikers.

point on any hike. This is a high-use area, so it is especially important to be conscious of your impact on the environment. Leave the area cleaner than when you arrived and avoid hiking in the delicate alpine meadows or cutting switchbacks. Backpackers seeking long-distance hikes in the Collegiate Peaks Wilderness Area can use this trail as a starting point. It winds on past Kroenke Lake for another one and one-half miles, ultimately connecting with Browns Pass Trail #1442.

The hike begins at the well-marked trailhead on the west end of the parking area. This heavily forested area provides an easy escape from the rush of everyday life. The well-maintained trail stays close to North Cottonwood Creek and is easy to follow. Follow the trail description for the Horn Fork Trail for the first two miles. At two miles you will reach the Forest Service sign directing you to either Kroenke Lake or Bear Lake. Take the left fork to Kroenke Lake. Here the trail enters a dense forest of mixed spruce and fir and begins the long, steady climb to Kroenke Lake.

At two and one-half miles, a sturdy three-log bridge carries you across Horn Fork Creek just before the confluence with North Cottonwood Creek. It's boggy in places, making hiking difficult at times but providing an abundance of flowers throughout the summer. Expect to be greeted in the next one-quarter mile with a variety of evergreen ground covers, a thick undergrowth of ferns, and waist-high flowers in midsummer!

The route follows along the base of Mount Yale, which is distinctly visible to the south. As walking begins to require more effort, conversations with hiking companions falter. There is a sense of sacredness along this trail. Cross an unnamed creek at 11,260 feet.

Don't give up during the last one-half mile of this hike. The destination is well worth the effort of the final, fairly steep stretch. This beautiful little alpine lake sits in a bowl beneath the northwest ridge of Mount Yale. Almost at timberline, it's surrounded by willows and provides numerous campsites for those wishing to pass the night.

If you plan to continue on, follow the trail due west along the south side of Kroenke Lake. Within a mile the route crosses the Continental Divide at 12,560 feet and begins a southerly traverse along a rocky trail that brings you to Browns Pass (12,020 feet) and Browns Pass Trail #1442. From here it is an easy two-and-one-half-mile descent to the Denny Creek trailhead on the Cottonwood Pass Road (County Road 306). A car shuttle would be required to return you to the North Cottonwood trailhead. Hikers interested in extended backpacking and exploration will turn north and begin the one-and-one-half-mile descent to Texas Creek Trail #416. The Texas Creek Trail extends west from this point toward Taylor Park, and northeast toward the Continental Divide. It intersects Pear Lake Trail #1461 and the Magdalene Gulch Trail, both of which may be followed over the Divide for an extended backpack.

May peace and peace and peace be everywhere.
                                    Mundaka Upanishads, I.1.

Frenchman Creek Trail #1457

Destination: *Frenchman Creek Headwaters*
Round-trip distance: *12 miles*
Starting elevation: *8,960 feet*
Maximum elevation: *12,200 feet*
Elevation gain: *3,240 feet*
Rating: *Difficult, but with good trail*
Time allowed: *1 to 2 days*
Recommended use: *Day hike, overnight, or extended backpack. Access to Mount Harvard and Mount Columbia. Connects to Pine Creek via South Pine Creek Trail #1458.*
Maps: *San Isabel National Forest; 7½' Mount Harvard; 7½' Harvard Lakes; Trails Illustrated Collegiate Peaks*

Trailhead Access

From the light at the intersection of U.S. Highway 24 and County Road 306 in Buena Vista, drive seven and one-half miles north on Highway 24 to the town of Riverside. Go west on CR386, passing through a gate at one-half mile. The road is steep and narrow through here but easily drivable in a two-wheel-drive car. At one and one-half miles you reach the Forest Service sign and a fork in the road. There is ample space to park here. Four-wheel-drive vehicles may continue on up to two miles from this point. The trail description begins here, as you begin hiking west up the left fork of the road.

Trail Description

This trail follows Frenchman Creek to its headwaters at 12,200 feet. It provides access to Mount Columbia and Mount Harvard from the east. This beautiful setting above timberline is not as heavily used as are some of the other trails on this side of the Collegiate Peaks Wilderness Area. The trail may also be used as part of an extended backpacking trip, because it connects with South Pine Creek Trail #1458,

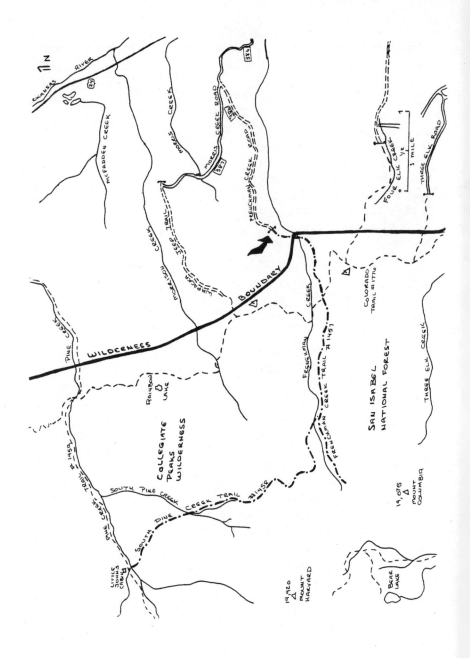

Frenchman Creek Trail #1457, South Pine Creek Trail #1458

which leads over to Pine Creek Trail #1459. Note that on some maps the Frenchman Creek Trail is called the "Harvard Trail."

Jeep roads are sometimes unappealing to hike along. However, this one is an exception. This narrow and occasionally steep road meanders west, carrying you through a variety of forest types: dense lodgepole pine wraps you in solitude; young stands of aspen form an arch to pass under; Douglas fir and spruce surround you as the road nears the Wilderness boundary. Just past a mile, the road leaves the lodgepole pine forest and tops out on a ridge, offering you an exceptional view of Marmot Peak to the east.

There is an open area for parking or camping at the edge of the Wilderness boundary at approximately two miles for those who have chosen to drive this far. The trail stays wide and pleasant beyond this point, crossing over to the south side of Frenchman Creek shortly after entering the Wilderness. Look carefully for the creek crossing. There is a highly visible tree dropped across the creek to the left. The stream is crossable via that tree, but crossing thus is treacherous. If you look to the right, you'll find a much better bridge and crossing point just behind a small stand of trees. Stay to the south of the stream for the remainder of the hike.

At a distance of three miles and an altitude of 11,200 feet, you'll cross the Colorado Trail (the old Main Range Trail), heading north and south. Continue hiking west, climbing at a fairly steady rate. Shortly past the intersection with the Colorado Trail, notice the large pile of pinecone duff on the left. This midden is created by the chickaree, or ground squirrel. Generations of chickaree will live in one tree, creating a pile of duff that is sometimes several feet deep. The chickaree often warns the other forest animals of your approach by his high rapid chattering as you pass by.

The trail levels off at three and one-half miles and becomes a little difficult to follow. Keep walking west. After crossing a boggy stream the way becomes obvious again.

A large talus field comes into view at about four miles. You are close to timberline now and will shortly top out on a ridge and round a bend. Mount Columbia is barely visible to the left. The trail will at times become quite indistinct, but there is little concern here. Simply stay on the south side of the creek, and up from the valley floor. You'll wind in and out of willow, occasionally finding, then losing the trail. Continue up the valley, eventually reaching the headwaters of Frenchman Creek. There are several excellent campsites here. This is one of the most beautiful sites in the Collegiates, an ideal home for marmots; they'll find your

The rock formation known as "The Rabbits," along the ridge between Mount Harvard and Mount Columbia.

presence and your pack interesting, so keep small items secure. Curious and friendly, they'll explore your pack and campsite with relative impunity.

West of the basin, on the ridge between Mount Columbia and Mount Harvard, is the rock formation aptly named "The Rabbits." The summit of 14,073-foot Mount Columbia is visible to the south. To climb Mount Columbia from your campsite in the basin, begin hiking almost due south, avoiding the steep rock at the base. Follow the gentle slope south, then southwest. Head for the east ridge, because you will approach the summit from that direction. The climb requires an altitude gain of less than 2,000 feet from the head of the basin. This is a relatively easy route over tundra, with some boulder-hopping in the final one-quarter mile. Return by the same route.

Mount Harvard (14,420 feet) may be climbed by hiking northeast from the basin initially. Gradually turn back toward the west, avoiding the steep rock slopes between Mount Harvard and Mount Columbia, and head up the gently sloping tundra. The summit will seem to be continually receding, but persistence will carry you across the one and one-half miles and 1,600 feet of elevation gain from the basin floor to the summit. Expect some rock-scrambling near the top. It's not difficult, but it will slow your progress.

Whether you are spending the night or returning the same day, stop and enjoy the waterfalls on the south side of the basin. The water pours gently over large flat rocks, an open invitation to dedicated sun worshipers.

But what is wisdom? Where can it be found? Here we come to the crux of the matter: it can be read about in numerous publications but it can be found *only inside oneself. To be able to find it, one has first to liberate oneself from such masters as greed and envy. The stillness following liberation — even if only momentary — produces the insights of wisdom which are obtainable in no other way.*

E. F. Schumacher
Small is Beautiful

South Pine Creek Trail #1458

(Refer to map on page 24.)

Destination: *Little Johns Cabin on Pine Creek*
One-way distance: *4 miles*
Starting elevation: *11,680 feet*
Maximum elevation: *13,080 feet*
Elevation gain: *1,400 feet*
Rating: *Easy*
Time allowed: *3 hours*
Recommended use: *Extended backpack. Connecting trail between Frenchman Creek Trail and Pine Creek Trail.*
Maps: *San Isabel National Forest; 7½' Mount Harvard; 7½' Harvard Lakes; Trails Illustrated Collegiate Peaks*

Trailhead Access

The South Pine Creek Trail connects the Frenchman Creek drainage to the Pine Creek drainage. The trail description is given as if one were

South Pine Creek from Mount Harvard's east shoulder.

hiking in from the Frenchman Creek trailhead, but it is as easily accessed from the Pine Creek trailhead.

To reach the Frenchman Creek trailhead, drive seven and one-half miles north of Buena Vista on Highway 24 to the town of Riverside. Go west on County Road 386. The road becomes rough at one and one-half miles, and two-wheel-drives must stop here. Four-wheel-drive vehicles may continue on up to two miles from this point.

The Pine Creek trailhead is reached by driving north thirteen miles from Buena Vista to the small town of Princeton (twenty-two miles south of Leadville). Turn west on County Road 388 and go .8-mile to a point where the road forks. Park and begin walking west along the right fork.

Trail Description

This trail would be used as part of an extended backpack, as a connecting trail between South Pine Creek and Frenchman Creek. It provides numerous possibilities for backpacking, some of which require a car shuttle. Follow the description for the Frenchman Creek hike (page 23). Just past four miles, when you break out of timber and round the bend into the valley, a faint trail appears on the north side of the creek. Watch carefully—it's difficult to see. The trail will gradually climb the north side of the valley. The maximum altitude of 13,080 feet is gained when you top the east saddle of Mount Harvard, visible from the valley floor of Frenchman Creek. From there you can look down into the Pine Creek valley, with Mount Oxford and Mount Belford visible to the north-northwest.

From the saddle you have several options. You may wish to simply enjoy the view, then return to the Frenchman Creek trailhead. Or, by following the curve of the saddle southwest and then west you can climb Mount Harvard, at 14,420 feet the third highest peak in Colorado. The climb from here is mostly over tundra, with some rock-scrambling necessary near the top. Technical ability is not necessary to climb this route, but be prepared for a full day of strenuous hiking.

If you are backpacking, follow the good trail down the north-facing slope of the saddle. This little-used trail becomes difficult to follow in the valley. Cross South Pine Creek at about one and one-half miles north of the saddle and begin working your way up and around the north-northeast ridge of Mount Harvard. The trail out of the South Pine Creek drainage is not easy to find but will top the ridge at about 12,000 feet. From this high point you can look northwest to the summit of 14,153-foot Mount Oxford. The trail, more clearly defined now, drops very steeply from the ridge through pine and spruce to Little Johns Cabin (10,800 feet) on Pine Creek.

An excellent three-day excursion would be to continue on along Pine Creek Trail #1459 two miles east from Little Johns Cabin to its intersection with the Colorado Trail. At this junction, take the Colorado Trail south three and one-half miles to the Frenchman Creek Trail crossing and then return along Frenchman Creek to your starting point. If you make preparations in advance for a car shuttle, a shorter hike is possible if you simply follow the good trail down Pine Creek as it winds generally east to the Pine Creek trailhead.

You may also turn left at Little Johns Cabin and hike three miles west along the Pine Creek Trail to Missouri Basin and the intersection with Missouri Gulch Trail #1469. From here the trail leads north over Elkhead Pass and into Missouri Gulch. This extended backpack would cover more than nineteen miles and pass five peaks over 14,000 feet along the way. A car shuttle would be required to return you to your originating trailhead.

The magnitudes of the mountains are so great that unless seen and submitted to a good long time they are not seen or felt at all.

John Muir
The Mountains of California

Pine Creek Trail #1459

Destination: *Silver King Lake*
Round-trip distance: *22 miles*
Starting elevation: *8,960 feet*
Maximum elevation: *12,640 feet*
Elevation gain: *3,680 feet*
Rating: *Difficult (because of distance), but with good trail*
Time allowed: *2 to 3 days*
Recommended use: *Extended backpack. Connects to Missouri Gulch Trail and South Pine Creek Trail. Beautiful area for hiking in the fall.*
Maps: *San Isabel National Forest; 7½' Mount Harvard; 7½' Harvard Lakes; Trails Illustrated Collegiate Peaks*

Trailhead Access

From the stoplight at the intersection of U.S. Highway 24 and County Road 306 in the center of Buena Vista, drive north thirteen miles on U.S. 24 to County Road 388 (twenty-two miles south of Leadville). Turn west onto this gravel road. Two-wheel-drives will only be able to go .8-mile to a point where the road forks. Plenty of parking space exists here. Four-wheel-drive or high-clearance vehicles may turn right at this fork, but the road is open to motorized vehicles for only a few hundred yards beyond this point.

Trail Description

This trail follows Pine Creek for eleven miles to one of its primary sources—Silver King Lake at 12,640 feet. Along the way it crosses the Colorado Trail #1776, South Pine Creek Trail #1458, and Missouri Gulch Trail #1469. This hike, like the Texas Creek area itself, is long if hiked all the way to the final destination. However, there are several points along the hike that make for an excellent day hike or a shorter backpack. The trail can also be used as part of a loop hike with any of the intersecting trails.

Park at the fork in the road and begin walking south along the road. At the top of a small rise fifty feet from the parking area, a tangle of roads sprouts in every direction. Bear right! Within a few hundred feet a sign announces your entry onto private property. No motorized vehicles may proceed beyond this point. Be prepared to pay a fee for each person, dog, or horse in your group. Due to willful and/or careless actions that have resulted in damage to livestock and property, the owners of this ranch are now asking all hikers who use their property as an access to the Wilderness to help defray the costs of damage.

The first one and one-half miles of this hike are along an old road. The first one-half mile passes through open meadow, offering views of the peaks at the head of the valley. The trail then moves closer to the stream, which is surrounded by fern and deciduous trees—a welcome alternative to the usual dense willows. Away from the water, the forest is principally ponderosa and lodgepole pine through this portion of the hike.

At approximately one mile you reach a generic sign that reads "Closed to All Vehicles," and the path narrows and begins a short, steep climb to the top of a low rise. Sign in at the Forest Service sign-in box, then enter a thick aspen forest. The trail follows through aspen or aspen and mixed conifer for the next two miles, making this an especially beautiful day hike in the fall. The route stays to the left of fast-flowing Pine Creek for the first four miles, moving away and above at times, then returning close to the banks. At approximately two miles, the trail moves away from the stream and begins climbing steeply up into the lodgepole pine forest. At the top of the short climb the creek rushes far below on the right, and the first open view of the valley since the beginning of the hike is available.

It's three and one-half miles from the trailhead to the Wilderness boundary, and another one-half mile to the intersection with the Colorado

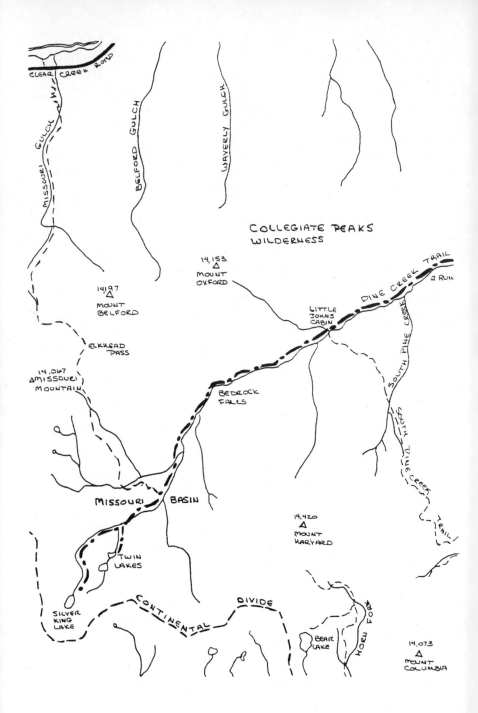

Pine Creek Trail #1459

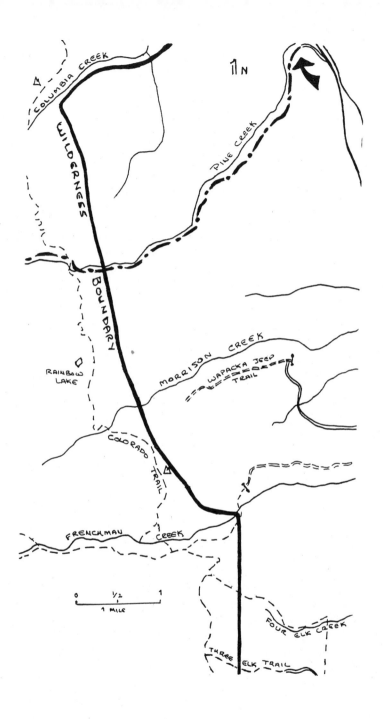

COLUMBIA CREEK

WILDERNESS

BOUNDARY

PINE CREEK

N

RAINBOW
LAKE

MORRISON CREEK

WAPACKA JEEP
TRAIL

COLORADO
TRAIL

FRENCHMAN   CREEK

0   ½   1

1 MILE

FOUR ELK CREEK

THREE ELK TRAIL

Trail. Here the Colorado Trail heads steeply up to the north and south, while the Pine Creek Trail crosses to the right side of the creek and continues on up the valley. This confluence of trails occurs in a wide, open meadow and makes a beautiful campsite. However, the area is in danger of being overused. If you can, plan to camp farther along the trail. Beautiful and private campsites exist throughout this valley, but please respect the pristine beauty here and follow standard wilderness practices. Camp no less than fifty yards from water. Use a campstove for cooking. If you must make a fire, be frugal with the wood, remembering that downed timber is home to many animals, insects, young trees, and other plants. When an area is used heavily for camping, the life cycles of the forest can be greatly affected.

The trail continues up the wide valley, following along the willowed banks of Pine Creek for two miles, moving in and out of the forest at the edge of the meadows. Active beaver ponds dot the entire stretch, providing good homes for trout. Fishing gear should be considered essential equipment on this hike! At two miles you reach Little Johns Cabin (10,700 feet). This area makes an excellent camp. Mount Oxford, at 14,153 feet, towers almost 3,500 feet above you to the northwest. Directly south of the main cabin and livestock area, the remains of a mine are tucked under the cover of the surrounding trees. Here, South Pine Creek Trail #1458 begins its steep climb up the northeast shoulder of Mount Harvard (14,420 feet). This less-used trail leads to the solitude of South Pine Creek, then on over the east shoulder of Mount Harvard to its connection with the Frenchman Creek Trail. An excellent three- or four-day trip can be made by following Pine Creek Trail west to the South Pine Creek Trail. From here, follow the South Pine Creek Trail south to the Frenchman Creek Trail. Hike east along Frenchman Creek to the Colorado Trail, then north to its intersection with Pine Creek Trail.

The well-used Pine Creek Trail continues west from the open meadow surrounding Little Johns Cabin, climbing through a dense mixed-conifer forest. Within one and one-half miles (seven and one-half miles from the trailhead) you reach Bedrock Falls at 11,200 feet. The level trail continues on an easy one and one-half miles, through open meadow and past beaver ponds, to its intersection with Missouri Gulch Trail #1469. This clear trail leads you southwest into Missouri Basin, over Elkhead Pass (13,200 feet), then into Missouri Gulch. Missouri Basin is wide, high, and open. If you're interested in following this route and are in fairly good condition, don't be intimidated by the altitude of Elkhead

Little Johns Cabin as seen from South Pine Creek Trail.

Pass. The trail traverses and switches back up the steep slope from the basin floor to the pass and is less difficult than one might imagine.

If you are following the Pine Creek Trail to its terminus at Silver King Lake, continue west, then south another two miles. If you are backpacking just to the lake, then returning, set your base camp near timberline and hike the final mile to the lake as a day hike. The boulder-strewn way is steep at times, and the delicate tundra at this altitude recovers slowly from our presence. For an extended trip requiring a car shuttle, a steep route exists over a low point along the Continental Divide, southeast of Silver King Lake. From the top, you can drop sharply down along loose scree and boulders to Magdalene Trail #542, one of the connecting trails to the Texas Creek Trail. This twenty-mile hike is generally easy and over good trail, with the exception of the climb over the Divide.

Let us put our minds together and see what we will make for our children.
Sitting Bull

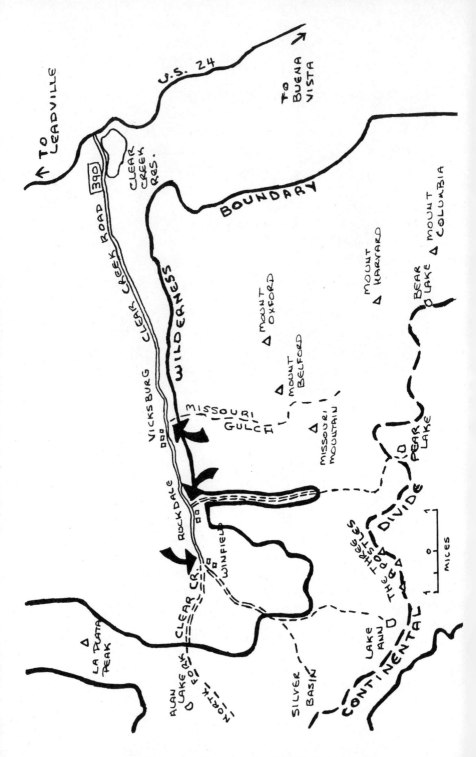

Collegiate Peaks Wilderness Area—Northeastern Portion

Hikes in the Northeastern Area

The hikes in this area are all reached from Clear Creek Road (County Road 390), a well-maintained gravel road that begins at Clear Creek Reservoir on U.S. Highway 24 midway between Leadville and Buena Vista. The road ends for two-wheel-drives at the historic town of Winfield, but four-wheel-drive vehicles may continue west or south for a few more miles to the Wilderness boundary. This popular area offers access to five of the eight 14,000-foot peaks that lie within the boundaries of the Collegiate Peaks Wilderness Area. The Clear Creek area is also popular with Colorado history buffs and modern-day prospectors, because several old mines, mining towns, and mining camps lie along this road and within the Wilderness boundary. You, too, may find yourself succumbing to "gold fever" as you explore the historic town sites and hike along the remains of the mining roads. The trails are generally well used and well maintained, and much wilderness hiking is available from a base camp well away from the main roads.

Missouri Gulch Trail #1469

Destination: *Elkhead Pass*
Round-trip distance: *9 miles*
Starting elevation: *9,660 feet*
Maximum elevation: *13,220 feet*
Elevation gain: *3,560 feet*
Rating: *Difficult, but with good trail*
Time allowed: *1 to 2 days*
Recommended use: *Overnight or extended backpack. Connects to Pine Creek Trail. Access to Missouri Mountain, Mount Belford, and Mount Oxford.*
Maps: *San Isabel National Forest; 7¹/₂' Mount Harvard; 7¹/₂' Winfield; Trails Illustrated Collegiate Peaks*

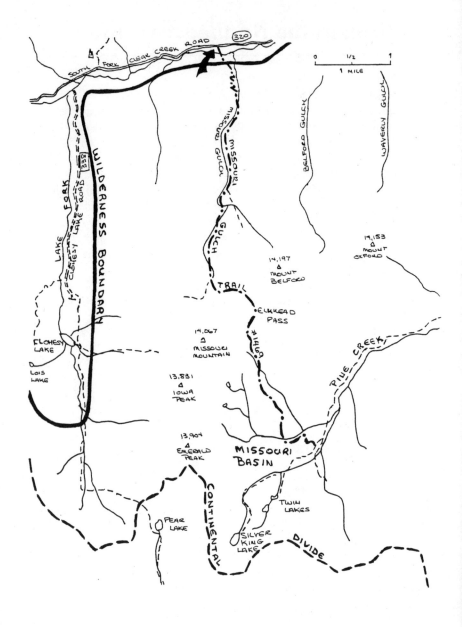

Missouri Gulch Trail #1469

Trailhead Access

Drive north from Buena Vista on U.S. Highway 24 for fifteen miles, or south from Leadville for nineteen miles, to Clear Creek Road. Follow this good gravel road eight miles west as it winds along Clear Creek. The parking area is on the south side of the road. This is the site of the old town of Vicksburg, and if you walk two hundred yards farther along the road you can view the restored historical buildings. Vicksburg was one of several major "cities" along Clear Creek, and one of the top mining camps in the 1880s. At its peak it had between two hundred and three hundred inhabitants.

Trail Description

Missouri Gulch is one of the more popular hiking areas in the Collegiate Peaks Wilderness. The well-maintained trail provides access to three peaks over 14,000 feet—Mount Oxford, Mount Belford, and Missouri Mountain. The trail heads almost due south, climbs over 13,200-foot Elkhead Pass, and drops down into Missouri Basin, where it intersects Pine Creek Trail #1459. The scenery is spectacular, ranging from dense pine forest to broad open meadows and high tundra. There's something subtly inviting about this area that beckons one to return again and again.

To begin the hike, walk south from the parking area. Cross Clear Creek using the well-constructed bridge and follow the clear trail. The trail starts gaining altitude rapidly with several switchbacks. The steep climb ends within a mile, and you enter a valley dense with willows. Expect daily rain showers here in July and August. If the day is warm and dry, you may enjoy walking through these willows in shorts. Not so dense as to impede your progress or hide the trail, they gently brush your legs as you pass through them. The trail becomes indistinct at times as you move higher in the valley. Stay east of the creek for the first two miles, then cross to the west side in a marshy area just below a steep, short climb. Continue on through this broad open valley, with only one more short steep climb, for another two and one-half miles to Elkhead Pass. Many beautiful campsites exist throughout the valley, but it's a fairly high-use area on delicate high-altitude ground. Camp well away from the trail and stream. Wood is scarce at this altitude, so plan to use a stove for cooking and layered clothing for warmth. Elkhead Pass is one of the highest named passes in Colorado. At 13,220 feet, it is the low point on

Camping in Missouri Gulch, at 12,500 feet (Elkhead Pass is in the background).

the ridge between Mount Belford and Missouri Mountain. Visible several miles southeast of the pass, across Missouri Basin, is 14,420-foot Mount Harvard.

If your intention is an extended backpack, follow the clear trail as it drops steeply from the pass into Missouri Basin. The basin itself is above timberline, so the trail occasionally fades in the marshy tundra. The trail crosses to the west side of a creek flowing down from the head of the basin. Head generally south and stay well to the west of the creek, avoiding the fairly steep drop-off along the southeastern edge of the basin. At the south end of Missouri Basin, the trail winds out of the broad basin into the forested Pine Creek valley and toward its intersection with Pine Creek Trail #1459, at 11,600 feet. From here, you may follow Pine Creek northeast for ten miles to emerge finally at the Pine Creek trailhead on U.S. Highway 24. Or, follow the Pine Creek Trail to South Pine Creek Trail, which leads south to Frenchman Creek Trail, which intersects the Colorado Trail. Either of these routes provides the option for an extended backpack through the area. See the trail descriptions for any of these hikes for more information on the routes.

From a base camp in Missouri Gulch you have access to climb three peaks over 14,000 feet. Mount Belford (14,197 feet) is easily climbed from Elkhead Pass. From the pass, climb east to Mount Belford's south ridge, then north to reach the summit. The climb is primarily over tundra, with some minor rock-scrambling at the top. From the summit of Mount Belford, you can see Mount Oxford (14,153 feet), one mile to the east. Mount Oxford may be climbed from here, but if you choose to continue on, watch the weather carefully and allow yourself at least two hours for the hike over and back. Thunderstorms can be expected in the early afternoon in the Colorado high country. These exposed peaks and ridges offer little protection from the weather, and you should be on your way down from the summit by noon or shortly after. The return from Mount Oxford requires a second climb of Mount Belford, then you must retrace your route back to Elkhead Pass. You may also return down the northwest slopes of Mount Belford, carefully avoiding the cliffs. The climb to Missouri Mountain (14,067 feet) from Elkhead Pass is not recommended. It is steep and treacherous, over loose rock. It is best approached from the trail approximately three-quarters of a mile northwest of Elkhead Pass. Climb southwest up the steep slopes, skirting the scree as much as possible, to attain the northwest ridge. Follow the ridge southeast to the summit. Return to the Missouri Gulch Trail by the same route.

I live, but I cannot live forever. Only the great earth lives forever, the great sun is the only living thing.

Crazy Dog, of the Kiowa

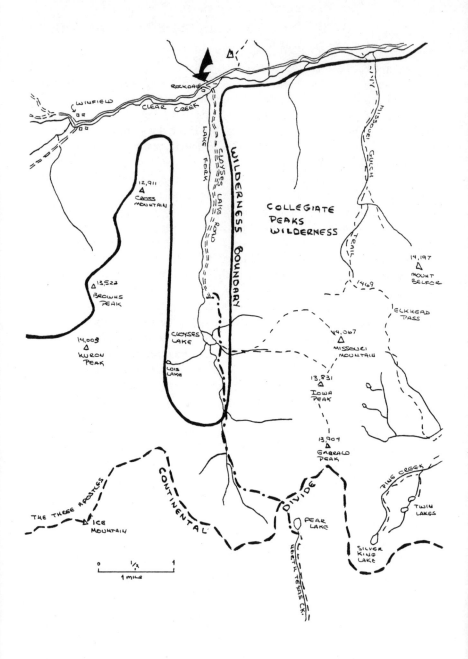

Pear Lake Trail #1461 (North)

Pear Lake Trail #1461, North

Destination: *Pear Lake*
Round-trip distance: *13 miles*
Starting elevation: *10,000 feet*
Maximum elevation: *12,100 feet*
Elevation gain: *2,100 feet*
Rating: *Difficult*
Time allowed: *1 to 2 days*
Recommended use: *Day hike, overnight, or extended backpack. Trail continues south to Texas Creek Trail (see Pear Lake, South, page 118). Access to Missouri Mountain, Iowa Peak, and Emerald Peak.*
Maps: *San Isabel National Forest; 7½' Winfield; Trails Illustrated Collegiate Peaks*

Trailhead Access

Drive north from Buena Vista on U.S. Highway 24 for fifteen miles, or south from Leadville for nineteen miles, to Clear Creek Road. Follow this good gravel road west for ten miles to Rockdale. This was once an active mining town, but all that remains today are a few restored cabins. The cabins are difficult to see as you drive by—watch carefully on the south side of the road. Turn left off Clear Creek Road, passing the cabins on the right. The road then drops down to the edge of Clear Creek, where two-wheel-drive cars must stop. Four-wheel-drive vehicles may continue south along this road for two and one-half miles before reaching the Wilderness boundary.

Trail Description

The hike description begins with the crossing of Clear Creek. There is no bridge here, and a creek crossing may not be possible early in the season during spring runoff. By midsummer the creek is wide and easy-flowing at this point. Bring an extra pair of shoes—the water's cold and the rocks are slick.

The road climbs steadily through a mixed spruce, pine, and aspen forest for the first mile. At approximately one mile you'll pass the remains of an old log cabin tucked under the aspen on the right. The road continues on, leveling out for the next mile and following along the willowed banks of Lake Fork Creek. At two and one-half miles you reach the Wilderness boundary, at the south end of an open meadow. This is a popular and well-used campsite for those who have driven this far. Fishing along Lake Fork Creek is excellent.

Sign in at the U.S. Forest Service sign-in box and continue on foot past the Wilderness boundary sign. Cloyses Lake sits on private land on the edge of the Wilderness, so take care to avoid trespassing. A sign will direct you to Huron Peak on the right and Missouri Mountain and the Lake Fork Trail on the left. If your destination is Pear Lake, turn left and follow the Lake Fork Trail. The well-defined trail skirts to the east of the private property, climbing quickly through a mixed spruce and fir forest. Near the south end of the lake the forest opens into a high clearing and the trail forks. No sign marks this fork, but the left fork leads up the steep slope to the saddle between Missouri Mountain and Iowa Peak. Take the right fork, which drops down to the south end of Cloyses Lake and begins following Lake Fork Creek.

You again enter a densely forested area as the trail follows closely along the east side of the creek. There is an incredible variety of flowers through here in midsummer—columbine, arnica, monkshood, elephantella, bluebells, and more colors of paintbrush than I have ever seen in one place.

Approximately one-half mile past the end of the lake, new trail has been cut. This new trail leads left up into the forest to avoid a boggy area that has formed. It soon rejoins the old trail just before entering a broad open meadow. If you are backpacking, this would make a beautiful campsite.

One mile south of Cloyses Lake, the trail crosses a stream and moves through willows and onto an "island" with streams flowing on both sides. The trail becomes faint at times but continues generally south. The stream on your left will drop away shortly, and you will continue to follow the main drainage on your right. Timberline and the Continental Divide are now visible ahead—a beautiful sight.

This was at one time a pack trail across the Continental Divide, and before then this route was probably used by the Mountain Utes. This relatively low spot on the Divide offers access to Texas Creek Trail #416 and, ultimately, Taylor Park on the south side (see Pear Lake Trail #1461, South, page 118). The trail is now obviously rutted by wagon wheels.

The snow-covered Continental Divide wraps around the end of the basin, dictating the direction of the trail.

Such damage to delicate tundra takes decades to restore. Follow along the tracks through spruce, fir, and willow as the trail gently gains altitude, finally reaching timberline at the end of the basin.

The route now turns to the east, following the contour of the Continental Divide, and begins to climb steeply out of the basin. The trees have become shortened and stunted in this harsh and fragile environment at timberline. The trail is difficult to follow at times as it weaves around the boulders and steep sections, climbing steadily to a wide high meadow. The route is not always easy to see directly ahead of you, but if you scan the mountainside you still see the marks of the wagon wheels left on the delicate tundra. Even if you lose the trail, the summit of the pass is obvious now, and once you reach the high point you'll look down four hundred feet to Pear Lake. No doubt where it got its name! The track continues down along the west side of the basin surrounding Pear Lake.

This high basin is beautiful beyond words. Here life is harsh and gentle at once. Tiny, tenacious purple flowers find a home in a small pocket of dirt on a granite boulder. Rockfall and the sound of water blend with the wind, echoing across the basin, the sound as hypnotic as that of ocean waves. The trail continues south from the lake, following along North Texas Creek and eventually connecting to the Texas Creek Trail. A loop backpacking trip can be made by hiking east from this point along the Texas Creek Trail to the Magdalene Gulch Trail. Follow the Magdalene Trail north, recrossing the Continental Divide south of Missouri Basin. From there you would hike north along the Missouri Gulch Trail to the Missouri Gulch trailhead on Clear Creek Road, two miles east of your originating point. (This hike is recommended for strong, experienced backpackers only, because the route over the Divide via Magdalene Gulch is steep and over loose rock.)

If you enjoy "peak-bagging," you may wish to climb Missouri Mountain, Iowa Peak, or Emerald Peak. Missouri Mountain is one of the eight peaks above 14,000 feet in the Collegiate Peaks Wilderness. Iowa and Emerald peaks are "centennials." Though not above 14,000 feet, they still rank among the one hundred highest peaks in the state.

A very strong hiker in good condition can climb Missouri Mountain (14,067 feet), Iowa Peak (13,880 feet), and Emerald Peak (13,904 feet) in one day. Follow the Lake Fork Trail to the south end of Cloyses Lake where the trail forks to the left up the mountainside. Climb steeply to timberline for one-quarter mile, then follow the contour northeast to gain Missouri's northwest ridge. Follow along the ridge southeast to the summit. From the summit of Missouri, drop directly south to the saddle between Missouri and Iowa. To climb the other two peaks, continue south, climbing 250 feet to the summit of Iowa. Emerald Peak is south another three-quarters of a mile. To descend, whether climbing Missouri alone or all three peaks, return to the saddle between Iowa Peak and Missouri Mountain. Drop steeply down the scree to regain the trail on the east side of Cloyses Lake. Make an attempt not to "ski" the scree. Sliding or skiing, even though it gets you to the bottom very quickly, causes considerable erosion and ultimately destroys the route for future hikers.

Though a sign points to Huron Peak (14,005 feet) just after the entrance to the Wilderness, another route exists from the South Fork Lake Creek Trail. If you wish to climb Huron from this side, refer to one of the guides listed on page 155.

Trees and stones will teach you that which you can never learn from the masters.

Saint Bernard

Lake Ann Trail #1462

Destination: *Lake Ann*
Round-trip distance: *11 miles*
Starting elevation: *10,250 feet*
Maximum elevation: *11,850 feet*
Elevation gain: *1,600 feet*
Rating: *Moderate (long, with some route-finding)*
Time allowed: *9 hours*
Recommended use: *Day hike, overnight, or extended backpack. Scenic area provides an opportunity for a long stay with numerous day hikes in the area.*
Maps: *San Isabel National Forest; 7½' Winfield; Trails Illustrated Collegiate Peaks*

Trailhead Access

Drive north fifteen miles from Buena Vista or south nineteen miles from Leadville on U.S. Highway 24 to Clear Creek Road. Turn west on this good gravel road and drive twelve miles to the old town of Winfield. In the center of Winfield the road forks, leading to the north and south. Take the south fork. Within one-half mile the road becomes impassable for most two-wheel-drive cars. Some four-wheel-drives may wish to continue on for two and one-half miles to where the road is closed. This is the same trailhead as for Silver Basin Trail (see page 51).

Trail Description

This scenic area provides an opportunity for a long stay with numerous day hikes in the area. The hikes range from easy to very difficult. From base camp along South Fork Clear Creek, you can hike to Lake Ann, Silver Basin, Harrison Flat, Browns Peak, Huron Peak, and the Three Apostles. Be forewarned that the Three Apostles offer some of the most difficult climbs in the area and require technical skill. The Lake Ann Trail will eventually be part of a Colorado Trail spur extending from Leadville to Gunnison.

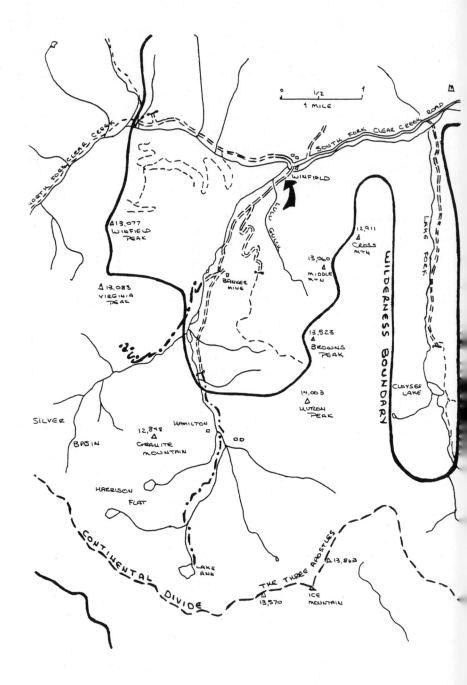

Lake Ann Trail #1462, Silver Basin Trail

The hike begins one-half mile south of Winfield, as you begin following the jeep road south. (Four-wheel-drive vehicles may continue south two and one-half miles to the Wilderness boundary.) The road follows along to the left (east) of South Fork Clear Creek through spruce and fir forest. This wide valley provides many beautiful campsites along the way, though signs of heavy use along the road are beginning to show. At approximately one-half mile, another four-wheel-drive road leads up the hill to the left. This is the route to Browns Peak. At one and one-half miles you pass the Banker Mine on the left. A road leads left to the Banker Mine and right toward South Fork Clear Creek. To reach Silver Basin, you would turn right at this point. To reach Lake Ann, continue south along the main road, staying on the east side of the creek. The area opens up now, and within another three-quarters of a mile you reach the Wilderness barrier, which halts vehicle traffic. The Three Apostles (Ice Mountain, West Apostle, and North Apostle) are visible directly to the south as soon as you enter the Wilderness Area. Walk along another mile through open meadow to a fork in the road at the old mining town of Hamilton. According to one source, Hamilton had more than three thousand miners in 1859, and the population doubled the following year. Little of it remains now.

A sign here directs you to the right, to Lake Ann. The left fork leads up to old mine ruins and is the start of a route to Huron Peak and the basin below the Three Apostles. To continue to Lake Ann, cross to the west side of South Fork Clear Creek via a sturdy log bridge and begin a steep climb through a dense forest of spruce and fir. The creek is now far below, where it has cut its path through cracks in the granite cliffs.

Within one-half mile you'll cross through an old avalanche path, and the Three Apostles break into view again. Shortly after crossing a stream on the south side of the avalanche run, the trail begins a set of three or four switchbacks up the side of the hill. Still west of the creek, the mountainside is so steep now that the creek is dropping through a series of waterfalls on its path down the valley. After a mile or so of this steep climbing, the trail enters an open meadow for the first time since the fork in the trail and the sign directing you to Lake Ann. The maps show the trail staying west of the stream all the way, but you actually cross to the east side soon after entering the open valley. The trail becomes obscure from time to time. The route continues directly south. You enter a boggy area out of the timber as you make the final approach to Lake Ann, and the only signs of a trail here may be the footprints of previous hikers left in the mud.

Lake Ann is one of the most beautiful lakes in the Collegiate Peaks Wilderness Area.

Lake Ann sits atop a small plateau at the far west end of the Three Apostles. The final approach is steep and dramatic. Angular granite slabs form stairstep waterfalls that terminate in a deep, crystal-clear pool. Are there water spirits playing here? It seems one can almost hear them laughing and singing. Perhaps it's just the sound of the water splashing on the rocks. Then again . . .

The setting of Lake Ann is breathtaking—a steep-sided cirque just below the Continental Divide. Directly to the east is the West Apostle and farther along the ridge is Ice Mountain, the highest and most difficult climb of the Three Apostles.

Harrison Flat can be seen to the northwest. The map shows a trail up there, which I suspect follows a steep waterfall rushing down into the basin below Lake Ann. Adventurous souls may wish to hike over and explore. However, this would require some bushwhacking through boggy willows and up a steep slope.

Two of the Three Apostles, Ice Mountain (13,958 feet) and North Apostle (13,863 feet), are termed "centennials." Though not above 14,000 feet, they are still among the highest one hundred peaks in the state. To reach the basin below the Three Apostles, take the left fork near the old town of Hamilton. Follow the road for a short distance, then cross a drainage that feeds South Fork Clear Creek. A faint trail exists on the east side of the creek. Staying to the east of the creek, bushwhack and climb gradually south into the basin below the Apostles (one and one-half miles). You can camp near tree line at 11,600 feet. The views from the basin are spectacular. Technical skills are required to climb the Apostles, but their awesome beauty can be appreciated by anyone.

A route to climb 14,005-foot Huron Peak begins approximately one hundred feet past the Wilderness boundary. Watch for cairn on the left and a faint trail leading three-quarters of a mile up a steep incline to the basin northwest of the summit. Another three-quarter-mile climb east out of the basin brings you to the saddle between Browns Peak and Huron. From here, head almost directly south along the ridge to the summit.

The world is not to be put in order, the world is order incarnate. It is for us to put ourselves in unison with this order.

Henry Miller

Silver Basin Trail

(Refer to map on page 48.)

Destination: *Silver Basin*
Round-trip distance: *7 miles*
Starting elevation: *10,250 feet*
Maximum elevation: *11,200 feet*
Elevation gain: *950 feet*
Rating: *Easy*
Time allowed: *5 hours*
Recommended use: *Day hike. Located near several historic mining towns.*
Maps: *San Isabel National Forest; 7½' Winfield; Trails Illustrated Collegiate Peaks*

Trailhead Access

Drive north fifteen miles from Buena Vista or south twenty miles from Leadville on U.S. Highway 24 to Clear Creek Road. Turn west on this good gravel road and drive twelve miles to the old town of Winfield. In the center of Winfield the road forks, leading to the north and south. Take the south fork. Within one-half mile the road becomes impassable for most two-wheel-drive cars. Some four-wheel-drives may wish to continue on for one and one-half miles to where the road is closed. This is the same trailhead as for Lake Ann Trail #1462 (see page 47).

Trail Description

This unusual hike will awaken the gold prospector sleeping deep within you. First, the only way to get here is by driving along Clear Creek Road past several historic mining towns. Take the time to stop and tour them. (I recommend reading the history of the area before visiting here. If you're unable to find books in your hometown, stop at the library or almost any store in Buena Vista or Leadville on the way.) If the tour of the mining towns doesn't arouse your prospector instincts, the sun glistening off chunks of iron pyrite along the trail surely will. This fool's gold will make you swear at times that you've found an undiscovered mother lode.

The hike begins one-half mile south of historic Winfield. A four-wheel-drive road leads south from here along the east side of South Fork Clear Creek through spruce and fir forest. This wide valley provides many beautiful campsites all along the way. If you are driving this road and plan to car-camp, avoid driving off the road and onto the grasses. Park as close to the road as possible and carry your camping equipment the few extra feet. The increasing use of this popular area is beginning to take its toll on the vegetation. At one-half mile the road forks, the left fork leading steeply up to Browns Peak. At one and one-half miles you reach the Banker Mine on the left. A road crosses your path here, leading left to the Banker Mine and right to Silver Basin. The main road continues south to the Wilderness boundary. From there you may hike to Lake Ann, as well as to several other scenic and challenging destinations. (See the Lake Ann Trail description on page 47.)

The first difficulty encountered is the crossing of South Fork Clear Creek, for no bridge exists. Though the creek is wide here, this can be a formidable challenge in early summer. Take along an extra pair of

The route to Silver Basin begins directly west of the ruins of the Banker Mine.

shoes—even in late summer the water is icy cold. The creek crossing is, fortunately, the only difficult part of this hike.

Once across the creek, follow the faint tracks of a road as it heads south, paralleling South Fork Clear Creek for a short distance. The road soon switches back to the right and begins a gentle climb past the remains of a mining operation, then turns again toward the south. High on the ridge above and to the right are the visible tailings remaining from the extensive mining in this valley during the late 1800s.

Approximately one-half mile past the creek crossing, nestled on a shelf well above South Fork Clear Creek, are a set of unexpected beaver ponds on the left. Continue southwest another one-half mile along the base of Virginia Peak. From this vantage point you get a breathtaking view of the entire valley. The Three Apostles stand majestically four miles to the south-southeast, along the Continental Divide; 13,523-foot Browns Peak rises to the east; Huron Peak (14,005 feet) towers 3,200 feet above you to the southeast; the steep slopes of Granite Mountain engage your view to the south; and, as you round the gentle southeast shoulder of Virginia Peak, Silver Basin comes into full view.

Continue along the road, which switches back to the north once before continuing its southwestern course. You'll follow the track for one-quarter mile to a second, gentle, curve in the road as it enters the edge of the forest. If you are adventurous and familiar with off-trail hiking, you may wish to break away from the road at this point and hike into Silver Basin. Though a trail appears on the Trails Illustrated map, no maintained trail exists here now. By following the faint game trails, however, and staying along the north side of the stream, you can make your way to the end of the basin. Carry the USGS topographic map for this area and a compass. Trace along the edge of the timber at 11,600 feet and begin working your way up into the basin, following the relatively gentle terrain.

If you continue on the road, it will begin a series of switchbacks, leading up the south side of Virginia Peak to 11,160 feet. The fever will surely come over you as you hike along this route, for the road is strewn with the iron-rich rock indicative of gold. The road ends abruptly—no mine shaft or buildings remain to indicate its original purpose. There seems no reason for this road but to have brought you here to admire the rock face of Granite Mountain directly to the south and to watch the black birds circling on the wind in the valley below you, their wings glistening white in the sun.

The described hike ends here, though if the day is young and the weather favorable, you may wish to continue on from this point to the summit of Virginia Peak, directly to the north and less than 2,000 feet above. Though one of the less-frequently climbed peaks in the area, at 13,088 feet it still provides a healthy challenge and the opportunity for a spectacular view of the valley. Return to camp by retracing your steps along the road.

Whatever you do may seem insignificant, but it is most important that you do it.

Mahatma Gandhi

North Fork Clear Creek Trail #1463

Destination: *North Fork Clear Creek*
Round-trip distance: *7 miles*
Starting elevation: *10,240 feet*
Maximum elevation: *10,900 feet*
Elevation gain: *660 feet*
Rating: *Easy*
Time allowed: *5 hours*
Recommended use: *Day hike. Hike begins at restored mining town of Winfield. Provides access to La Plata Peak.*
Maps: *San Isabel National Forest; 7½' Winfield; 7½' Mount Elbert; Trails Illustrated Collegiate Peaks; Trails Illustrated Crested Butte/Pearl Pass*

Trailhead Access

Drive north fifteen miles from Buena Vista or south twenty miles from Leadville on U.S. Highway 24 to Clear Creek Road. Turn west on this good gravel road and drive twelve miles to the old town of Winfield. In the center of Winfield the road forks, leading to the north and south. Take the north fork. Two-wheel-drive cars may proceed west for another one-quarter mile before the road becomes impassable. Some four-wheel-drives may wish to continue on for one mile to the Wilderness boundary.

Trail Description

Winfield, founded in the early 1880s by a mule, was one of the major mining cities along Clear Creek Gulch. The story goes that some prospectors heading for Gunnison country camped along Clear Creek one night. Their mules wandered off during the night, and when the prospectors went to search for them in the morning they found gold float in the creek. Within weeks several camps had sprouted. Winfield and Vicksburg (four miles east) emerged as the top camps, with two hundred to three hundred residents each by the mid-1880s. Today the buildings of both towns are maintained as historic sites.

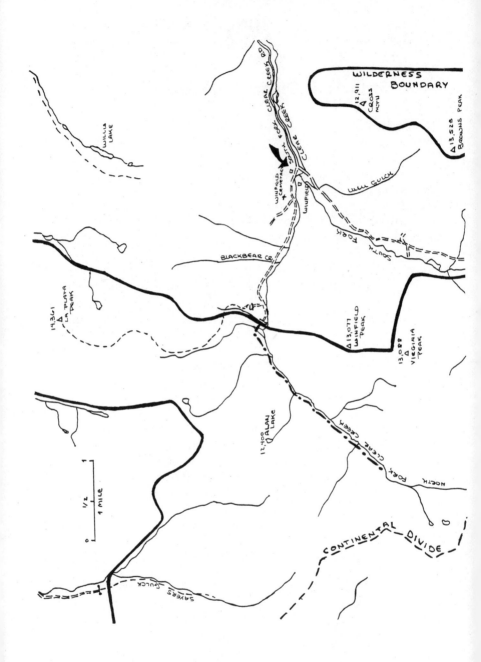

North Fork Clear Creek Trail #1463

Looking southeast toward Browns Peak and Huron Peak (at the center of the photo) from North Fork Clear Creek Road.

Begin hiking north from Winfield along an old mining road. The road turns west within a few hundred yards, where it continues on past the Winfield graveyard on the right. The flat terrain and easy winter access make this an excellent cross-country ski trail. Follow the route along the North Fork Clear Creek through open meadow. Aspen covers the hillside on the right and potentilla virtually carpets the valley floor for the entire hike. On the mountainside to the south another old mining road switches sharply up toward a minor peak just east of Winfield Peak.

At about one and one-quarter miles the road branches. Continue west along the main road, ignoring the right branch. Here La Plata Peak comes into view to the north for the first time. The valley broadens out now, and within one-half mile you reach the Wilderness boundary. Throughout this portion of the hike La Plata and the route up to its southwest shoulder are visible to the north.

The valley stays broad and the elevation gain gentle as you continue on toward the headwaters of the North Fork Clear Creek. The trail remains to the right of the creek and the marshy willows along its banks. Though still well below timberline, the trees are becoming sparse through here. At approximately two miles into the hike you enter a forest of mixed spruce and fir. Monkshood is waist-high here, and the potentilla still carpets the valley in places.

At three and one-half miles you pass the steep drainage from Alan Lake. The climb to the lake from this point would be difficult, with a lot of bushwhacking. If you wish to visit Alan Lake, an easier approach might be to begin traversing the hillside one-half mile east of the drainage, working your way up the 1,400 feet more gradually.

The trail up the valley continues through similar terrain, becoming increasingly faint as you go along. There is no true destination on this hike. Continue as long as you wish, and return when you are ready. Enjoy this quiet valley. With the exception of the "local natives"—ground squirrel, deer, porcupine, and coyote—you will most likely be alone.

If you wish to scale 14,361-foot La Plata Peak, climb north from North Fork Clear Creek just before entering the Wilderness Area. The trail is easier to find on the way down from the summit than on the way up, but it's critical to stay east of the drainage and continue almost directly north. Many hikers have gotten into the wrong basin, only to discover their error as they ascend a ridge and view La Plata far off and inaccessible from where they stand. One and one-quarter miles after leaving the North Fork Clear Creek Trail, head northeast for one-quarter mile, then north again for a final steep climb over snow and loose rock to La Plata's southwest shoulder. From here it's a relatively easy mile of rock-scrambling and bouldering northeast to the summit.

To those who have entered them, the mountains reveal beauties they will not disclose to those who make no effort. This is the reward the mountains give to effort. And it is because they have so much to give and give it so lavishly to those who enter them that we learn to love the mountains and go back to them again and again . . . The mountains reserve their choice gifts for those who journey into them and stand upon their summits.

Sir Francis Youngblood

Hikes in the Northern Area

Independence Pass Road (Colorado Highway 82), which extends from Aspen to Twin Lakes Reservoir on U.S. Highway 24, gives access to the set of hikes in the northern section of the Collegiate Peaks Wilderness. Many of these trails and the roads to them are popular for late-spring and early-summer skiing. The high altitude, heavy snow, and winter road closure all combine to offer fresh, untracked skiing well into the summer. Even in August an occasional "ski bum" or the characteristic S-shaped tracks can be seen high in the couloirs or on the snowfields. With the exception of Difficult Trail and Weller Lake, which are close to Aspen, and La Plata Trail, which leads to La Plata Peak, this area receives slightly less use than the more easily reached trails along Cottonwood Pass Road, Clear Creek Road, and U.S. Highway 24.

La Plata Trail

Destination: *La Plata Gulch*
Round-trip distance: *6 miles*
Starting elevation: *10,200 feet*
Maximum elevation: *11,400 feet*
Elevation gain: *1,200 feet*
Rating: *Easy*
Time allowed: *5 hours*
Recommended use: *Day hike or overnight backpack. Easy-to-reach basin with numerous beautiful campsites. Approach to La Plata Peak.*
Maps: *San Isabel National Forest; 7¹/₂′ Mount Elbert; 7¹/₂′ Independence Pass; Trails Illustrated Independence Pass*

Trailhead Access

From Leadville, drive south fifteen miles on U.S. Highway 24 to Colorado 82 (Independence Pass Road). Follow this paved road west,

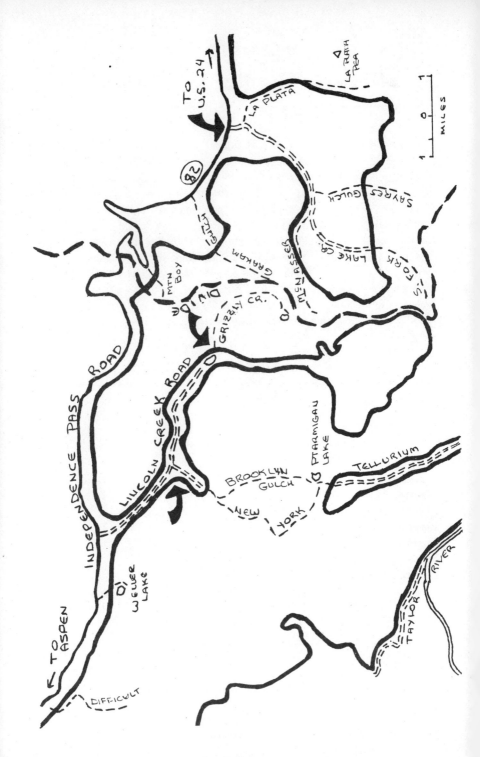

Collegiate Peaks Wilderness Area—Northern Portion

passing through the scenic resort town of Twin Lakes. Within two miles the road begins following Lake Creek up the valley. Approximately eight miles past Twin Lakes, turn south on County Road 391—this is the South Fork Lake Creek Road. To reach CR391 from Aspen, drive east thirty miles on Colorado 82. The drive from Aspen offers the opportunity to view Ellingwood Ridge and La Plata Peak from a better vantage point than you will have later as you hike along the base of the north ridge of La Plata.

There is private property along the first one and one-half miles of County Road 391. Please honor the No Parking and Private Property signs. Generous parking space is available at the intersection of Highway 82 and CR 391, and the well-marked trailhead is just .3-mile south of the parking area.

Trail Description

Used primarily as an access to La Plata Peak, this hike also offers excellent camping and fishing. The first one and one-half miles are fairly steep, but at about 11,000 feet the grade lessens and the valley widens, providing numerous beautiful campsites to those who have persevered.

The first quarter-mile of this hike, once you leave South Fork Lake Creek Road, is nothing short of spectacular. A mining town once existed at the intersection of Colorado 82 and County Road 391, and a few of the cabin remains can still be seen slightly off the trail to the north. Named Everett after the founder, C. M. Everett, this town had some thirty houses, three mills, several stores, and a few hotels in 1882. There were many mines in the area, and Everett's mills processed much of the ore. It was one of the most important stops on the stage run from Leadville to Aspen. When the mining faded and the railroad came to Aspen, the pass fell into disuse and Everett was abandoned. Step back in time as you pass and imagine what it must have been like here during those early years of mining.

Keep your head up as you walk this first one-quarter mile. The spectacular two-mile-long Ellingwood Ridge stands majestically in front of you, slightly to the southeast. The ridge is a popular and challenging climb for avid mountaineers who relish the opportunity to repeat Albert Ellingwood's conquest of La Plata Peak in 1921 via this route. Directly ahead of the trail is the northwest ridge of La Plata Peak. The trail will follow the drainage below this northwest ridge and the ridge directly to the south.

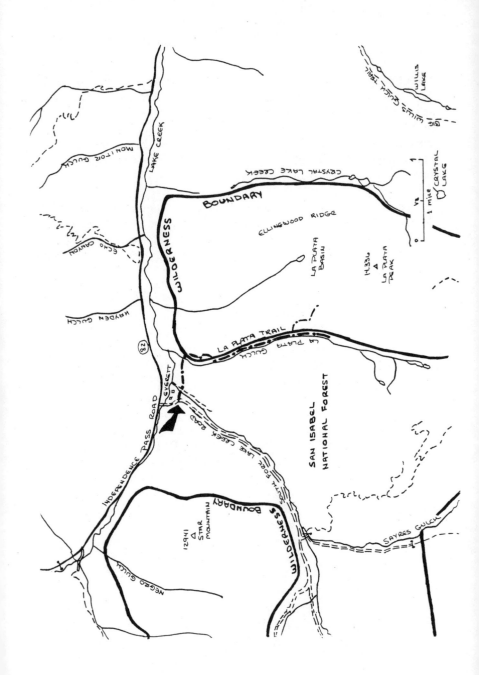

La Plata Trail

The log bridge across South Fork Lake Creek spans white water ten feet below.

The first creek crossing may be somewhat intimidating to those un-comfortable with fast-moving water and heights! If that is the case with you, don't look down as you cross a sturdy three-log bridge slung ten feet in the air above South Fork Lake Creek. The trail climbs steeply up from the stream crossing for thirty feet, then levels off and continues a gentle meandering through aspen and pine. Another one-quarter mile brings you to a log bridge laid across the La Plata Gulch drainage; this one's not nearly as exciting as the previous creek crossing.

Immediately after crossing this stream, the trail makes a sharp turn to the right (south). Ignore the faint trail heading east. This is the old trail to La Plata Basin, and though flagging can still be seen on the trees, the trail is no longer maintained by the Forest Service. Now the hike begins. The trail becomes steeper and steeper for the next mile. The forest is dense, the area is rugged, the creek rages down the drainage. You'll pass rock outcroppings off to the right from time to time. Their primary purpose seems to be to offer a place to rest awhile and listen to the water-song rising up from the creek.

The trail to La Plata Peak (14,361 feet) breaks off from the main trail at about two miles and heads east up the northwest ridge. After a steep climb of 1,600 feet, the summit is a mile to the south. Those inter-ested in climbing this peak should consult one of the climbing guides listed on page 155 before attempting it.

This subalpine location (just after the trail levels out and before timber-line) is an excellent site to set up camp. Large flat areas exist above the streambed and are surrounded by clusters of spruce and fir. From this base camp you can climb La Plata or hike farther up the valley to fish and sight-see. The main trail continues for a short distance but soon becomes faint in the rocks and willows. You may continue following the drainage for an-other mile, finally reaching the unnamed alpine lake at 11,800 feet.

This trail is well cairned, flagged, and heavily used during July and August. If you seek solitude, go early or late in the season. I hiked this trail on Memorial Day weekend and found amazingly little snow (during a heavy snow year) and no other hikers. If you do hike at that time of year, be prepared for sudden storms. You may have the good fortune I experienced and find only sunshine, water-song, and animal tracks ahead of you in the snow.

Did you know that trees talk? Well they do. They talk to each other, and they'll talk to you if you listen. Trouble is, white people don't listen. They never learned to listen to the Indians so I don't suppose they'll listen to other voices in nature. But I have learned a lot from trees: sometimes about the weather, sometimes about animals, sometimes about the Great Spirit.

Tatanga Mani (Walking Buffalo)

South Fork Lake Creek Trail #1466

Destination: *Headwaters of South Fork Lake Creek*
Round-trip distance: *15 miles (5 miles if you drive to Wilderness boundary)*
Starting elevation: *10,200 feet*
Maximum elevation: *12,300 feet*
Elevation gain: *2,100 feet*
Rating: *Difficult (long, but with good trail)*
Time allowed: *1 to 2 days*
Recommended use: *Day hike or backpack. Could be part of an extended backpack into Lincoln Creek or Red Mountain Creek. Rugged and remote.*
Maps: *San Isabel National Forest; 7½' Independence Pass; 7½' Pieplant; Trails Illustrated Crested Butte/Pearl Pass; Trails Illustrated Independence Pass*

Trailhead Access

From Leadville, drive south fifteen miles on U.S. Highway 24 to Colorado 82 (Independence Pass Road). Follow this paved road west, passing through the scenic resort town of Twin Lakes. Within two miles the road will begin following Lake Creek up the valley. Approximately eight miles past Twin Lakes, turn south on South Fork Lake Creek Road 391. Standard automobiles must park at the intersection of Highway 82 and CR391. Four-wheel-drive or high-clearance vehicles may follow this road southwest for five and one-half miles to the Wilderness boundary. County

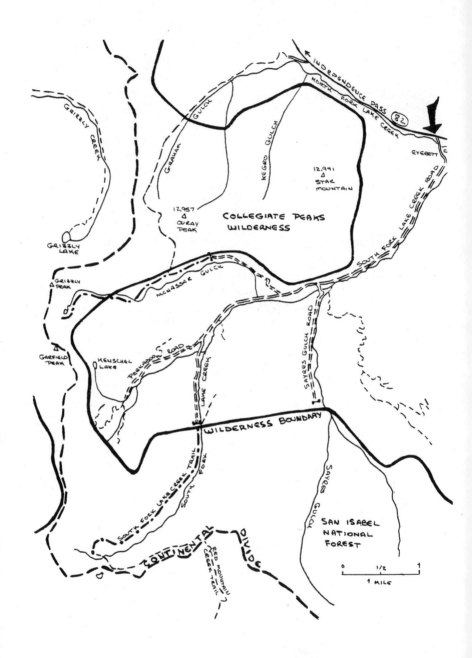

South Fork Lake Creek Trail #1466, McNasser Gulch Trail

Road 391 can also be reached by driving east from Aspen on Colorado 82 for thirty miles, crossing Independence Pass.

Trail Description

County Road 391, which intersects Highway 82 east of the winter gate closure, provides an excellent place for cross-country skiing in the winter and spring. In the summer and fall, this gentle road along South Fork Clear Creek invites mountain bikers to follow it to the Wilderness boundary. Here they may stash their bikes or lock them to the gate and continue on foot up the valley.

The four-wheel-drive road winds through aspen and pine, gaining a mere 1,000 feet in five and one-half miles. With the exception of one or two extremely rough spots (the first occurring in the first half-mile), the road could be driven in a standard two-wheel-drive. Hiking here is a delight, requiring little effort. Begin early though, because this area is generally open with little tree coverage, and by midday the way is hot and dry. There are numerous campsites along the creek, but be aware of and respect the private property that occasionally dots the valley.

In Spanish, *colorado* means "color red," and you'll understand how this state got its name as you hike up the road after it passes McNasser Gulch at three miles and before it reaches Peekaboo Gulch. The mineral-laden water of the South Fork Lake Creek runs through a bed of red rock. Iron has washed down the sides of the mountains, painting them brilliant red and gold. Red Mountain stands out along the Continental Divide, its northeast shoulder separating McNasser and Peekaboo gulches.

At four and one-half miles along the road you'll pass the fork up Peekaboo Gulch. On the map a four-wheel-drive road one and one-half miles southwest along Peekaboo Gulch climbs steeply up to the Wilderness boundary. Another hiker informed me that Henschel Lake, in the basin north of Red Mountain and just outside the Wilderness boundary, is accessible from there. From farther up South Fork Lake Creek you can turn around and see an old mine road that branches off the Peekaboo Gulch road, switching sharply up the mountainside to the mining sites. Even today these mines are occasionally active, their activity following the vagaries of the human spirit and the price of gold.

Just past the fork to Peekaboo Gulch you pass private property and two cabins on the right. At one time this road was used as a stage road to Aspen, and the smaller of these cabins was a stage stop along the way.

An apparently abandoned log cabin sits on the left side of the creek

Trout were top-feeding in this unnamed lake just below the Continental Divide at 12,000 feet. This photo was taken from the basin at the end of South Fork Lake Creek Trail.

at five and one-quarter miles. A road, blocked by a gate, leads across to it. Continue south on foot along the main road past the Wilderness boundary. This little-used route gradually narrows as it winds its way up into the basin, staying high above the thick willows surrounding the South Fork Lake Creek.

Within one-half mile of the Wilderness boundary, Lake Pass becomes obvious to the south. Though a trail appears on the 7½-minute Pieplant map, there is no visible route to Lake Pass from this vantage point. There are signs of a faint trail near the top leading over to connect with Red Mountain Creek Trail #543.1 (see page 125). To get there from directly across the basin, however, would require bushwhacking through about one-half mile of dense willows, then climbing over 800 feet to attain the 12,200-foot pass.

At approximately seven miles (one and one-quarter miles past the Wilderness boundary), a faint road forks to the right and begins switching back up to the north. Stay on the main road, heading generally southwest, then west.

The road becomes wide again as you approach the end of the basin. The earth recovers slowly at this altitude and the old wagon ruts cut deeply. Once around the bend near the end of the basin, the road can be seen traversing up the north end of the basin, where it disappears in rock and snow near the top. Here the old stage route crosses the Continental Divide and drops down into the basin at the headwaters of Lincoln Creek, passing the ghost town of Ruby and the remains of the Ruby Mine.

High in the basin, the faint remnants of a road lead across the tundra to the south. This may well be the last remaining trace of the route over Lake Pass and into Taylor Park. I did not pursue that possibility but instead rested awhile 200 feet above an alpine lake in which numerous native cutthroat trout were top-feeding.

My hike ended here, where I explored the awesome beauty and solitude of this high alpine meadow. Remnants of roads beckoned, and I followed them here and there, peering down first into one then another basin. I had come unprepared for an overnight stay, however; so, turning, I retraced my steps down the valley. Following the ghosts of generations of men and women who had come along this route before, I could not help wondering what *their* mission and purpose in passing through here had been.

We use the word wilderness, but perhaps we mean wildness. Isn't that why I've come here? In wilderness I seek the wildness in myself and in so doing come on the wildness everywhere around me. Because, after all, being part of nature I'm cut from the same cloth.

Gretel Ehrlich
"Waterfall"

McNasser Gulch Trail

(Refer to map on page 66.)

Destination: *McNasser Gulch*
Round-trip distance: *11 miles*
Starting elevation: *10,200 feet*
Maximum elevation: *12,400 feet*
Elevation gain: *2,200 feet*
Rating: *Difficult*
Time allowed: *9 to 10 hours*
Recommended use: *Day hike or backpack. Could be hiked as part of an extended stay along South Fork Lake Creek.*
Maps: *San Isabel National Forest; 7½' Independence Pass; Trails Illustrated Independence Pass*

Trailhead Access

From Leadville, drive south fifteen miles on Highway 24 to Colorado 82 (Independence Pass Road). Follow this paved road west, passing through the scenic resort town of Twin Lakes. Within two miles the road will begin following Lake Creek up the valley. Approximately eight miles past Twin Lakes, turn south on South Fork Lake Creek Road 391. Standard two-wheel-drive autos will park at the intersection of Highway 82 and CR391, while four-wheel-drive vehicles may follow this road southwest for three miles to McNasser Gulch Road. The McNasser Gulch Road continues for one and one-quarter miles to a gate. From this point until it enters the Wilderness Area near the end of the basin it is a private road, open only to hiking. County Road 391 can also be reached by driving east from Aspen on Colorado 82 for thirty miles, crossing Independence Pass.

Trail Description

The first three miles of this hike is along County Road 391, a gentle four-wheel-drive road. The road winds up the valley, following South

The view southwest along McNasser Gulch Trail.

Fork Lake Creek. By the time you reach the turnoff to McNasser Gulch you will have gained less than 600 feet in elevation. At three miles the road branches to the right, just past a dense stand of spruce and aspen. This is an excellent place to stop and rest before beginning the hike up into McNasser Gulch.

After a short, steep climb, the road into McNasser Gulch begins twisting through a cool spruce forest. The forest is open at times, offering exceptional views of the South Fork Lake Creek valley to the west and south. Within the first mile of the fork from CR391 (South Fork Lake Creek Road), you'll cross two streams coming down from the north, the water falling through open space high above you and to the right. On the left and fifty feet below, an unnamed creek rushes past. Fed by the melting snow from Grizzly and Garfield peaks on the Continental Divide, it sings its praises of the forests and flower-covered meadows it has passed on its journey. Thick patches of bluebells rise up in the coolness of the forest cover. At just over four miles (one mile past the McNasser Gulch turnoff) you reach a gate on the west end of a lush field of bright yellow sunflowers. The road from here to the Wilderness boundary is private, but hiking (only) is allowed.

One-quarter mile past the gate, you enter a high meadow. Water plunges down the steep rocky slopes on the right, the sound echoing across the valley. This water feeds the thick carpet of grasses, wildflowers, and willows, which will nourish elk for the next few months. On the left, a vertical scree slope drops down from a ridge, the trees marching along the top to timberline. Near the end of the meadow, one-quarter mile farther on and just before entering the last stand of trees in the valley, you pass a private cabin on the right. At the end of this stand of trees are the very faint remains of a pack trail heading north to skirt around Ouray Peak and drop down into Graham Gulch.

The road forks just before entering wilderness, both forks leading to privately owned and occasionally active mines. Leave the road here and continue west, following along the north side of the stream. The route climbs steeply for a short distance, then begins a gentle traverse around the basin, passing below 13,988-foot Grizzly Peak on the right. This centennial peak was first climbed from this side. The hike ultimately ends at an alpine lake in the rocky cirque below Garfield Peak. You'll meet few other hikers in this high basin tucked quietly back under the protective circle of the Continental Divide.

No pain here . . . no fear of the past, no fear of the future . . . no petty personal hope or experience has room to be . . .

John Muir
The Mountains of California

Mountain Boy Gulch

Destination: *Mountain Boy Park*
Round-trip distance: *3 miles*
Starting elevation: *11,500 feet*
Maximum elevation: *12,160 feet*
Elevation gain: *660 feet*
Rating: *Easy*
Time allowed: *2 to 3 hours*
Recommended use: *Day hike. Good late-spring skiing. Easy hike to basin above timberline.*
Maps: *San Isabel National Forest; 7½' Independence Pass; Trails Illustrated Independence Pass*

Trailhead Access

From Leadville, drive south fifteen miles on U.S. Highway 24 to Colorado 82 (Independence Pass Road). Follow this paved road twenty-two miles west to the hairpin curve southwest and just below Independence Pass. Independence Pass Road is closed through this section during the winter months. Mountain Boy Gulch can also be reached by driving east from Aspen on Colorado 82 for twenty-two miles.

Trail Description

This is a favorite late-spring and early-summer ski area. Backcountry skiers come to enjoy the deep untracked snow in this basin as soon as Independence Pass Road is open. In the summertime, however, it's rarely used. Perhaps the reason for this is that there is no trailhead marker or maintained trail here. Don't let this stop you from enjoying this little-used area, though. It's an easy place to get above timberline quickly, where you can enjoy the beauty and solitude of a high basin. There is ample parking available on the north side of the road.

The most difficult part of this hike is the short stretch of bushwhacking through willows at the beginning. Follow close to the creek, which heads south from the bend in the road. This route seems to offer the

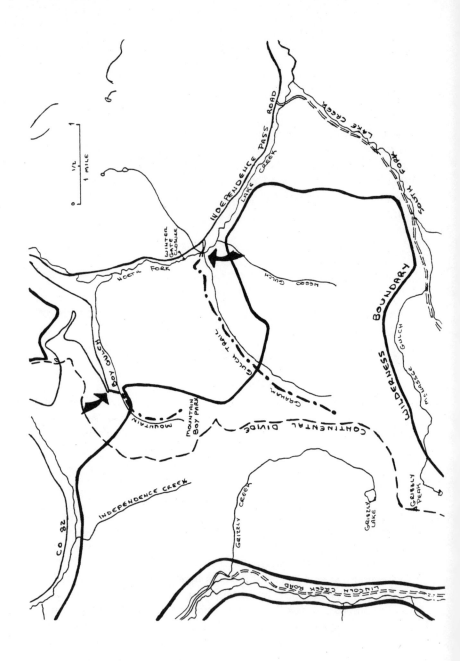

Mountain Boy Gulch, Graham Gulch Trail #1478

Even in June the snow is deep and untracked in Mountain Boy Gulch.

least resistance to your passage. Though the willows grow close to the water's edge, there is room for you to pass by, and the ground is less marshy than through the denser willows in the open.

When you reach the small ridge running along the east edge of the stream flowing out of Mountain Boy Park, turn southwest and begin following this drainage, staying on the north side of the creek for a short distance. There is no trail here. Cross to the low ridge above and to the east of the creek. There really is no "correct" way to pass through this section. Your main goal should be simply to avoid the willows. Stay in the forested area along the ridge until well past the densest area of willows.

As the valley begins to turn south, work your way up from the valley floor and away from the creek. Here the faint remains of an old mining road emerge. At one point you may come across the crumbling remnants of a log corduroy: a ribbed "bridge" laid down on the ground beneath the marshy willows. You quickly reach timberline and the road climbs even higher up the side of the gulch, moving well above the willows. The route stays below the krummholz (a German word translated as "crooked wood"), the twisted and stunted conifers that grow close to the ground at timberline.

There is no concern about losing the way here, even though the trail is faint. Just follow the drainage all the way into the basin, staying high and to the left. It is beautifully quiet once out of the trees and away from the road. High in the basin you reach Mountain Boy Park—an alpine meadow covered with flowers during the peak of summer. Here you find the remains of an old mining operation. The ruins of two cabins provide protection from the weather—a place to rest, eat lunch, and speculate on the past. On the left of the basin the route traverses up to a low point on the saddle; on the right the tracks switch back up the side of the steep basin to the Continental Divide. High above the basin to the south, a path traverses through the loose rock toward what appears to be bore holes on the rocky cliffs.

The time given for this hike is two hours, but if the weather is good you will want to stay for a day, isolated from the noise and rush of the "civilized" world. Plan to spend some time exploring the surroundings. You can easily hike to the low shoulder east of the basin. With a little more effort climb northwest, then north to the Continental Divide. And, of course, there's always the option of just sitting quietly and simply enjoying the beauty, solitude, and peace of this alpine park.

The clearest way into the Universe is through a forest wilderness.
John Muir

Graham Gulch Trail #1478

(Refer to map on page 74.)

Destination: *12,600-foot pass*
Round-trip distance: *7 miles*
Starting elevation: *10,520 feet*
Maximum elevation: *12,600 feet*
Elevation gain: *2,080 feet*
Rating: *Moderate*
Time allowed: *9 to 10 hours*
Recommended use: *Day hike. Good fishing at trailhead. Good cross-country ski area. Trail gets light use in summer.*
Maps: *San Isabel National Forest; 7½ ● Independence Pass; Trails Illustrated Independence Pass*

Trailhead Access

Drive south fifteen miles from Leadville or north twenty miles from Buena Vista on Highway 24 to Colorado 82 (Independence Pass Road). Follow this paved road west, passing through the town of Twin Lakes. At approximately seventeen miles, turn left on an improved dirt road, crossing North Fork Lake Creek within .2-mile. The road ends very soon after the creek crossing, becoming trail. The trailhead, on the eastern side of the Continental Divide, can also be reached by driving east from Aspen for thirty-six miles on Colorado 82. Turn right .2-mile east of the winter gate closing.

Trail Description

The outlet near the trailhead is a popular fishing spot, and numerous campsites are available. This is also a popular winter backcountry ski trail. The trail is accessible all winter because the trailhead is just east of the winter gate closing for Independence Pass Road.

Begin hiking northwest along an old mining road. A spectacular view of La Plata Peak and Ellingwood Ridge is available to the southeast just

La Plata Peak (on the left) and Ellingwood Ridge, as seen from Graham Gulch.

before you enter the forest. The route remains heavily forested for the first one and one-half miles, with only momentary breaks from time to time. The remnants of the mining operation are somewhat disturbing throughout this hike but are also a good reminder of the necessity for us to "walk gently on the earth." Still, much timber remains—primarily tall, stately spruce. This is a mixed spruce and pine forest, with few wildflowers during the first half-mile.

At approximately three-quarters of a mile you'll cross a steep drainage, dry even as early as mid-July. This will be the first break in the dense forest and an opportunity to look southeast once again to La Plata Peak and Ellingwood Ridge. Pass an old log cabin on the right within one hundred feet. The trail now passes close to the shallow creek on the left. The proximity of this creek and another creek crossing contributes to the abundance of tiny wild strawberry plants through here.

The trail has climbed quite steeply since the beginning, gaining 600 feet in less than a mile. The road now switches back sharply, moving away from the creek. The route continues climbing through a few switchbacks before once again returning to the side of the stream. The continuation of the road is visible to the southeast across the drainage. The road continues on south along the stream for another one-quarter mile before crossing the drainage, however.

At approximately two miles the road crosses the main stream and switches back to the northeast. The trail into the basin is virtually non-existent, but the final destination is within view. Climb northwest up the steep hillside, just enough to get well above the willows. From here you can traverse southwest one mile to a point where you will finally connect with the remains of an old pack trail. Follow this trail southeast then south for one-half mile to the 12,600-foot saddle on the west shoulder of Ouray Peak. If you still have a little energy left, the rocky summit of 12,957-foot Ouray is one-quarter mile east, with an elevation gain of 350 feet.

This was one of the many routes across the Continental Divide used by early prospectors and settlers. If, after traversing the basin, you had turned northwest instead of southeast, you would cross the Divide after a short but steep climb of one-quarter mile. From here you could drop sharply down onto Grizzly Lake Trail #1990 and out to the Lincoln Creek Road. This could be an interesting extended backpack, requiring a car shuttle. From the Lincoln Creek Road one can connect to New York Trail #2182, which leads southwest toward Taylor Park. Alternately, by hiking southeast from Ouray's west saddle one could connect with South Fork Lake Creek Trail #1466. Either of these hikes would be a true wilderness experience, for portions of these trails are rarely used.

Within you now are divine ideas for caring for our Earth and our global family . . . You have everything it takes to make a difference! We are one, after all, you and I.

Teilhard de Chardin

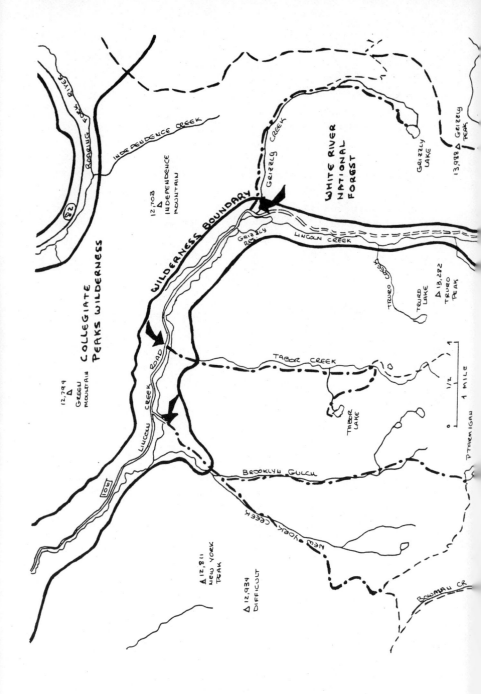

Grizzly Lake Trail #1990, Tabor Creek Trail #2185, New York Trail #2182,
Brooklyn Gulch Trail

Grizzly Lake Trail #1990

Destination: *Grizzly Lake*
Round-trip distance: *7 miles*
Starting elevation: *10,560 feet*
Maximum elevation: *12,515 feet*
Elevation gain: *1,955 feet*
Rating: *Moderate*
Time allowed: *7 to 8 hours*
Recommended use: *Day hike. High-use area, so be especially conscious of your impact on the environment.*
Maps: *White River National Forest; 7½' Independence Pass; 7½' New York Peak; Trails Illustrated Independence Pass*

Trailhead Access

Follow Highway 82 (Independence Pass Road) for ten miles east from Aspen to the Lincoln Creek Road on the right. Go six miles south and east up Lincoln Creek Road 106 to Grizzly Reservoir and then one-half mile toward the Portal Campground. The trailhead is located in the trees just past the dam (before reaching the Portal Campground), directly above the caretaker's residence, and on the left side of the road. You may park on the left, just past the trailhead.

Trail Description

The Grizzly Lake Trail is an easy-to-follow hike. It's an excellent place to see wildlife and offers fairly good fishing. This moderately easy trail takes you along the base of the Continental Divide to a deep alpine lake located above timberline at 12,515 feet elevation and right at the base of 13,988-foot Grizzly Peak, the fifty-fifth highest peak in the state. There are many wildflowers along the route in the latter part of the summer, and fishing in the lake for cutthroat trout is fairly good. Remember that the lake will still be frozen early in the summer because of the elevation. The lake is partially surrounded by a number of rock slides extending into the water from the steep sides of the encircling peaks, so exercise

The view west from Grizzly Lake Trail.

care along the shoreline. Be prepared for sudden afternoon thunderstorms at this high elevation. You'll be above timberline for one to two
hours at least.

The trail to Grizzly Lake follows Grizzly Creek most of the way. Begin
hiking steeply up through a fragrant spruce forest, accompanied by the
roar of Grizzly Creek on your right. Within the first one-half mile the trail
emerges from the dense tree cover and the forest opens out into a high
open meadow. The trail, surrounded by rocky, barren peaks, levels out.
It passes in and out of meadow and forest as it climbs gently along the
north side of Grizzly Creek.

At about two miles the route passes through the final stand of spruce.
Here the trail passes an old log cabin on the left, then drops down into
a field of columbines and mixed wildflowers along Grizzly Creek. There
are no bridges across Grizzly Creek, so just choose a narrow spot and
hop across the rocks. The trail has been following along the west side
of the Continental Divide for the last mile, and now it wraps around to
the west just as the Divide wraps around to meet Grizzly Peak. To the
east and 1,200 feet above the trail, a wide grassy saddle is one of the
relatively few places where one can cross the Divide. A climb to the saddle

would give you access to Graham Gulch Trail #1478 (see page 77), lead-ing northeast to Colorado 82 (Independence Pass Road).

Shortly after crossing Grizzly Creek, the trail begins a steady climb through sparse willows. The route gradually gets steeper, offering you a series of "false summits." Time and again the trail appears to approach the lake on top of a plateau. And time and again you top a steep climb only to be greeted by an expanse of tundra and the trail continuing across to another "final" climb. This can be discouraging to those unaccustomed to the illusions of the mountains. Here and there along this last mile of trail, hikers pause to rest and contemplate whether to continue. The lake is not visible until you are nearly to it.

The true final stretch works its way around and up a rocky cliff, then heads toward a shelf with a snow cornice in the background. The last one-half mile consists of crossing through a marshy meadow, then taking a long traverse cut into the side of the mountain. Patches of snow remain around the lake all summer, and its deep blue color hints of the water's temperature, just barely above freezing. Still, cutthroat trout flourish in this icy environment, and a few intrepid fishermen surround the lake and test their skill against these hardy natives.

I'd rather wake up in the middle of nowhere than in any city on earth.
Steve McQueen

Standing on the snow-covered shores of Grizzly Lake in early August.

Tabor Creek Trail #2185

(Refer to map on page 80.)

Destination: *Tabor Lake*
Round-trip distance: *6 miles*
Starting elevation: *10,200 feet*
Maximum elevation: *12,300 feet*
Elevation gain: *2,100 feet*
Rating: *Moderate*
Time allowed: *5 to 6 hours*
Recommended use: *Day hike. High-use area. Could be included as part of an extended camping and fishing trip along Lincoln Creek.*
Maps: *White River National Forest; 7½' New York Peak; Trails Illustrated Independence Pass*

Trailhead Access

Drive east out of Aspen on Highway 82 (Independence Pass Road) for ten miles to Lincoln Creek Road 106. Turn right and follow this road 4.2 miles to the trailhead parking lot on the right (south) side of the road. The road is narrow and rough for the first three miles. Colorado Highway 82 may also be reached by driving south from Leadville on U.S. Highway 24 for fifteen miles to Highway 82. Follow Highway 82 west for thirty-four miles to Lincoln Creek Road 106. The trailhead is accessible by standard two-wheel-drive passenger cars, but the road is rough.

Trail Description

This moderate hike follows Tabor Creek, ending at 12,300-foot Tabor Lake. One could also follow the trail to a 12,480-foot pass at the end of the basin that looks into Galena Creek. Tabor Lake sits in a cirque one-half mile west and 900 feet above Tabor Creek. Expect beautiful, rugged, and rocky scenery.

There are two campgrounds and numerous campsites along the Lincoln Creek Road. The first, Lincoln Gulch Campground, is one-half mile from Highway 82. The second, Portal Campground, is at the end of the road near the Grizzly Reservoir. Managed campsites are also available along the first three miles of the Lincoln Creek Road. The well-marked Tabor Creek trailhead is 4.2 miles along Lincoln Creek Road, tucked a few hundred feet off the road among the trees. Adequate day parking is available here, but no overnight camping is allowed.

Begin walking southeast from your car along the rocky remains of a road. Within 150 feet you reach Lincoln Creek. From this vantage point look directly across the creek. Hidden in the willows on the other side is the continuation of the trail. Lincoln Creek cannot be easily crossed here, but if you turn left and walk upstream a short distance you'll find a wide, sturdy tree dropped across the water. Return downstream on the other side, watching carefully on your left for the unmarked beginning of the trail. If you miss the trail initially, just stay to the left (east) of the dry rocky drainage coming down from Tabor Creek.

The trail climbs steeply through a dense forest for approximately one-quarter mile to its intersection with the road following the New York Collection Canal. This canal collects Western Slope waters that are then carried to the Front Range via a canal passing beneath the Continental Divide. The route here is obvious. A wooden bridge with railings carries you across the canal, and a Forest Service sign points the way.

Follow along for a short distance on the east side of Tabor Creek. You cross to the west side within fifteen minutes of passing the canal. Tabor Creek flows heavily for most of the summer. The well-maintained and easy-to-follow trail rises gently and, though not at timberline yet, soon breaks out into the open. This trail seems not to be as heavily used as is the Grizzly Lake Trail just a few miles farther along Lincoln Creek Road, but it is equally beautiful.

Some of the most interesting features of this hike are the many remains of avalanche runs. The mountainside to the west is covered with sparse vegetation and must be just the right angle for snowslides. Even in early August the deep remains of the snowslides fill the creek basin below the trail. The icy waters of Tabor Creek run down from the high basin, cutting a path and disappearing below the snow. Stay on the trail as you cross the avalanche paths: Circling above or below the snow causes multiple paths to form. A natural phenomenon visible here is the red color of the snow. This is caused by a species of algae that had adapted to these cold high-altitude conditions. In summer, as the snow melts, the algae reproduce in numbers large enough to color the snow red. The snow may even taste like watermelon in places where the algae is unusually prolific, and occasionally your footprints will be blood red behind you.

The low point on the horizon is the final destination for those choosing to hike to the end of the basin above Tabor Creek.

The trail climbs gently, passing through one or two columbine meadows. At one and one-half miles you'll enter a small spruce forest (11,100 feet). The trees are sparse, stunted, and windblown but provide just enough protection for a flower garden to flourish. Bluebells, purple penstemon and monkshood, brilliant pink paintbrush, and numerous varieties of yellow flowers fill your vision.

At two miles you pass a waterfall high and to your right. This is the lower waterfall from Tabor Lake. Continue on for a short distance, past the dense patch of spruce, to a point where the slope becomes less steep (11,600 feet). A faint trail breaks off to the right and begins traversing back to the northwest. The view is breathtaking as you climb above the valley floor and turn to look at the steep barren slopes to the east.

As the terrain levels out, begin moving in a more northerly direction. High on the cliffs a finger of rock seems to point the way to Tabor Lake. *Up!!* Keep that point in sight as you continue on. Soon, the upper waterfall from Tabor Lake breaks into view. Water falls through space, the rock painted black from its continual contact with the icy water. The way is steep. The trail appears, finally, snaking its way up along the north side of the waterfall. In spite of the steepness of the trail, the awesome beauty of the waterfall beckons you on.

Take heart. Within half an hour you'll be sitting beside a high alpine lake. You won't see the lake until you're almost to it. Deep blue-green water, a protective circle of cliffs, and the sound of the water falling away behind you are your rewards for this day's efforts. Return to the trailhead by the same route.

If you wish, you may continue on up the valley, past the point where you turn west to Tabor Lake. Many hikers prefer this longer hike, eight miles round trip, to the unnamed pass at 12,480 feet. The faint trail weaves back and forth across the basin, following the lay of the land around the rock outcroppings until the final steep climb at the end of the basin.

It is not what you do, but what you stop doing that matters.
Nisargadatta Maharaj

New York Trail #2182

(Refer to map on page 80.)

Destination: *Pass at forest boundary*
Round-trip distance: *8 miles*
Starting elevation: *10,140 feet*
Maximum elevation: *12,280 feet*
Elevation gain: *2,140 feet*
Rating: *Moderate*
Time allowed: *9 hours*
Recommended use: *Day hike or backpack. Possible loop hike with Brooklyn Gulch. Possible extended backpack into Taylor Park (requiring a car shuttle).*
Maps: *White River National Forest; 7½' New York Peak; Trails Illustrated Independence Pass*

Trailhead Access

Follow Highway 82 (Independence Pass Road) east from Aspen approximately ten miles to Lincoln Creek Road 106. Turn right (south) on this improved dirt road and drive about three miles to the New York Trail turnoff (107) on the right. To reach Lincoln Creek from U.S. Highway 24 running north and south between Leadville and Buena Vista, drive west from Twin Lakes Reservoir thirty-four miles on Independence Pass Road.

Trail Description

The first one and one-quarter miles of this hike is the same as for the Brooklyn Gulch hike. It begins by crossing Lincoln Creek via a sturdy two-log bridge. The route follows an old mining road as it ascends steeply through a mixed conifer forest. Continue along the steep road for a little over one mile to its intersection with the service road for the New York Collection Canal. This canal collects Western Slope water that is ultimately transported under the Continental Divide to Lake Creek (along Independence Pass Road) and the Twin Lakes Reservoir. A sign at the intersection directs you south to the continuation of the trail.

One-quarter mile along this level road brings you to a sharp switchback in the road and the Brooklyn Gulch Trail. Continue along the road as it curves around the nose of the broad ridge separating Brooklyn Gulch from New York. Within another quarter-mile a trail sign on the left marks the turnoff to the New York Creek Trail. One hundred feet beyond this point the road ends abruptly at the concrete dam diverting the waters of New York Creek.

At the trail sign, turn left off the service road and begin following a clear trail through a mature spruce and fir forest. The trail climbs above the dam, staying high and to the left of the creek. You'll pass through a short stretch of open meadow before moving back into dense timber. At two miles the trail forks. Take the right fork, which drops down to the side of New York Creek. No bridge exists, but if you walk upstream a short distance the creek narrows and you can jump across the rocks. The path climbs steeply away from the stream for a short distance, winding around tall mounds of dirt (the remains of an old mining operation?) now covered with grasses and flowers. The trail has entered a broad open valley and begins a gentle climbing traverse of the mountainside. It continues this traverse, switching back from time to time and gradually moving away from the creek. At three miles the route begins turning to the west

New York Trail is well marked with posts and cairn above timberline.

and enters another forest of mixed spruce and fir. The sound of water can be heard off to the left, though this stream may not be flowing late in the summer.

After climbing steeply for another half-mile, the trail crosses to the south side of the stream and begins traversing up a steep slope and bending toward the south. The trees fall away as you approach 12,000 feet, and the basin comes into full view. Patches of stunted spruce decorate the hillocks dotting this high basin.

The path continues its steady climb to the south. The trail is faint but well used, and post and cairn mark the way across the wide, high valley. One-quarter mile to the south the trail can be seen climbing over the rocky tundra to the low point on the ridge surrounding the basin. This 12,280-foot pass stands on the boundary between the Gunnison and White River national forests.

Several great day hikes are available in and around this basin. From the saddle one can hike southeast across the high tundra-covered ridge to Ptarmigan Lake. Hike north from the lake over a rocky pass and drop into Brooklyn Gulch. Plan on a strenuous ten-mile hike, with three miles of it above timberline.

An easier loop hike into Brooklyn Gulch retraces the New York Trail to 11,900 feet, then turns southeast across the tundra toward an unnamed lake at the head of New York Creek. From here, begin hiking northeast, staying above the timber and heading up along the ridge separating New York and Brooklyn. Drop down into Brooklyn Gulch to connect with the faint trail leading north along the creek.

In early fall, when the threat of early-afternoon thunderstorms is past, one could hike west from the saddle and, staying high on the broad ridge, continue hiking all the way around this high basin. At the low point northeast of the basin, just before ascending the 12,925-foot peak south of Difficult Peak, drop back into the basin to regain the trail.

If you are prepared for an extended backpacking trip requiring a car shuttle, continue south from the 12,280-foot pass to connect with the Bowman Creek Trail. This trail leads south to the far end of the Taylor River Road.

These are by no means the only potential day or extended hikes in this valley. A short study of the map or the horizon from the pass will open up numerous others. One could return to this high basin several times and still not exhaust all the possibilities.

Coming down from the mountains to men, I always feel a man out of place; as from sunlight to mere gas and dust, and am always glad to touch the living rock again and dip my head in high mountain pastures.

John Muir
The Mountains of California

Brooklyn Gulch Trail

(Refer to map on page 80.)

Destination: *Pass at forest boundary*
Round-trip distance: *8 miles*
Starting elevation: *10,140 feet*
Maximum elevation: *12,600 feet*
Elevation gain: *2,460 feet*
Rating: *Moderate*
Time allowed: *9 hours*
Recommended use: *Day hike or backpack. Could be used as a loop trip with New York Trail. Possible extended backpack into Taylor Park (requiring car shuttle).*
Maps: *White River National Forest; 7½' New York Peak; Trails Illustrated Independence Pass*

Trailhead Access

Drive east out of Aspen on Highway 82 (Independence Pass Road) approximately ten miles to Lincoln Creek Road 106. Turn right (south) and drive 3.2 miles to the New York Trail turnoff on the right (Road 107). Ample parking exists at the trailhead. Camping is available at the Lincoln Creek campground or along the first three miles of Lincoln Creek Road. Highway 82 may also be reached by driving south from Leadville on U.S. Highway 24 for fifteen miles. Go west for thirty-four miles to Lincoln Creek Road 106. This is the same access as for New York Creek Trail #2182.

Trail Description

Begin by crossing Lincoln Creek via two logs that have been cabled together. Follow an old mining road as it ascends steeply through a dense and tall forest of mixed conifers. The road climbs more steeply than one expects from a road of this sort. At about a mile you'll cross through the remains of an avalanche run. Young spruce are beginning to reforest the area. This opening offers you the opportunity to turn and view the Lincoln Creek valley you have just climbed above. Within a few hundred yards you reach the road that follows along the New York Collection

A faint trail follows along the banks of the stream flowing through Brooklyn Gulch.

Canal, 600 feet above the trailhead. Turn right (south). A sign points the way to the continuation of the trail.

Another three hundred yards along this level road brings you to a sharp switchback in the road and the Brooklyn Gulch drainage into the New York Canal. The road continues on past here to New York Trail. To hike into Brooklyn Gulch, leave the road and step over the small dam and begin following an indistinct trail close to and on the east side of the creek. It's green and lush through this part of the hike. Bluebells flourish in this environment. I put on rain pants to pass through the hip-high dew-covered foliage.

Approximately two miles from the beginning of the hike, cross over to the west side of the stream. The faint trail crosses from one side to the other of the creek, and you may lose it at times. Just stay close to the water and continue on up the valley.

Within another three-quarters of a mile the valley opens up and the end of the basin comes into view. The trees become sparse as you approach timberline. The trail is extremely faint at times. Stay on the right (west) side of the stream. You'll surely want to avoid the impenetrable willows on the left! The trail finally disappears in the willows on the right.

Walk above the willows, into the edge of the forest, to reconnect with the trail.

At 11,200 feet the trail almost completely disappears. For much of the time I followed matted grass from the previous passage of—another person? an animal? I don't know. I saw neither the day I hiked here. Though the road along Lincoln Creek had been crowded with fishermen, bikers, hikers, and sunbathers, no one else ventured up Brooklyn Gulch on that day.

Cross to the east side of the creek at about 11,300 feet. The trail climbs steeply for a short distance along the edge of a sparse spruce forest. Within one-quarter mile the route moves out of the cover of trees. The final one mile gains 800 feet in elevation, the most difficult stretch of the hike. Watch the weather carefully as you climb up to the pass above Ptarmigan Lake. Lightning, wind, and hail are usual components of the standard early-afternoon thunderstorms at this altitude. Plan to be on your way back down from the high point of 12,600 feet by noon.

This hike could be combined with New York Trail #2182 (see page 88) to make a long day hike or an overnight backpacking trip. A faint trail continues south, over the Continental Divide, to 12,300-foot Ptarmigan Lake. From there the trail climbs to a pass directly west of the lake. The route continues northwest over rough terrain, staying above 12,000 feet for the next two miles. Due to the high altitude, occasionally rough terrain, and route-finding required, this would be a difficult, challenging, and very interesting hike. The hike is slightly easier if begun in New York Gulch with the return hike down Brooklyn Gulch.

Toward calm and shady places I am walking on the Earth.

                                                                Ojibwa song

Difficult Trail #2196

Destination: *Difficult Trail*
Round-trip distance: *7 miles*
Starting elevation: *8,160 feet*
Maximum elevation: *9,500 feet*
Elevation gain: *1,340 feet*
Rating: *Easy*
Time allowed: *6 hours*
Recommended use: *Day hike. Easy access from Aspen. High-use area.*
Maps: *White River National Forest; 7½' Aspen; 7½' Hayden Peak; Trails Illustrated Independence Pass*

Trailhead Access

Drive east from Aspen for approximately four miles along Colorado 82 (Independence Pass Road). The entrance to Difficult Campground is on the south side of the highway. Follow this side road one-half mile to a parking area on the right. The well-marked trailhead is in the back left corner of the parking area.

Trail Description

Less than four miles from Aspen, this popular trail is convenient and well used by local residents and out-of-state visitors alike. It offers excellent views of the town of Aspen and an opportunity to see the remains of cabins from the mining days in this area.

The trail begins on the north side of the Roaring Fork River. A well-constructed bridge drops you off on the south side of the river where, due to the heavy use of the area, trails sprout in several directions. Note outstanding landmarks and clusters of trees here, for you may experience some difficulty finding the cutoff to the bridge again when you return. An obvious trail soon emerges among the sagebrush and scrub oak and begins a gentle southerly ascent.

As you move across the flat terrace at the beginning of the hike, the sound of the Roaring Fork fades behind you and is replaced by the

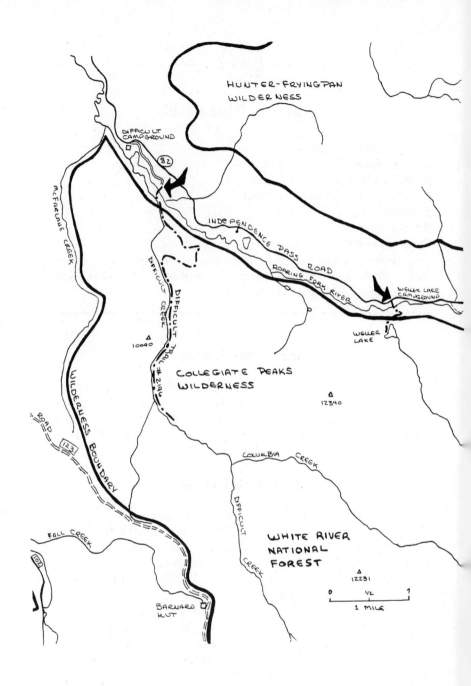

HUNTER-FRYINGPAN
WILDERNESS

DIFFICULT
CAMPGROUND

82

McFARLANE CREEK

INDEPENDENCE PASS ROAD

ROARING FORK RIVER

WELLER LAKE
CAMPGROUND

WELLER
LAKE

DIFFICULT CREEK

DIFFICULT TRAIL #2196

△ 10090

COLLEGIATE PEAKS
WILDERNESS

△ 12340

WILDERNESS BOUNDARY

ROAD 123

FALL CREEK

105

COLUMBIA CREEK

DIFFICULT CREEK

WHITE RIVER
NATIONAL
FOREST

△ 12231

BARNARD
HUT

0   1/2   1
1 MILE

Difficult Trail #2196, Weller Lake Trail

The trail along Difficult Creek is still snow-covered in late May.

roar of Difficult Creek. The trail follows Difficult Creek south for one-half mile to a point where the creek flows northeast out of a steep ravine and the trail veers off sharply to the southeast. As the sound of the roaring creek tapers off, it is replaced by the sounds of the trees and wildlife. There is a steady breeze through here, and the variety of trees presents an orchestra of instruments for the wind to play upon. The gentle soprano of the young aspen echoes the bass of the tall ponderosa pine. The trees, Earth's lungs, breathe in and out as the wind passes through them, singing and dancing at once. The chattering of the chickaree interrupts the wind and the tree-dance, leaving space in the air for the answering birdsong. This celestial music accompanies you for the next half-mile, beckoning you to rest and listen for a while. The trail then begins a steep climb—first east, then south, then west—and after two and one-half miles re-connects with the thundering chorus of Difficult Creek as it rushes over boulders and fallen trees.

Follow the creek as far as you wish. The unmaintained trail becomes increasingly difficult to follow, finally forcing a retreat. But not without first reminding us of the essential wildness of this Earth and our place within it.

Your task is not to seek for love, but merely to seek and find all of the barriers within yourself that you have built against it.

A Course in Miracles

Weller Lake Trail

(Refer to map on page 96.)

Destination: *Weller Lake*
Round-trip distance: *2 miles*
Starting elevation: *9,360 feet*
Maximum elevation: *9,560 feet*
Elevation gain: *200 feet*
Rating: *Easy*
Time allowed: *2 hours*
Recommended use: *Day hike. Easy hike, close to Aspen. High-use area.*
Maps: *White River National Forest; 7½' New York Peak; Trails Illustrated Independence Pass*

Trailhead Access

To reach the Weller Lake Trail from Aspen, drive east on Colorado 82 (Independence Pass Road) for approximately seven miles. From Leadville, drive south fifteen miles on U.S. Highway 24 to Colorado Highway 82. Follow this paved road west for thirty-six miles.

The Weller Lake Campground is on the left (north) side of the road. The trailhead is on the south side of the road. There is ample parking available at the trailhead.

Trail Description

The close proximity to Aspen and easy access make this an excellent hike for local residents and out-of-state visitors. Camping is available at

Weller Lake, just seven miles east of Aspen.

the beautiful (though small) Weller Lake Campground. The trail begins just east of the winter closing gate, so access is possible only in the summer.

Although the time allowed is given as two hours, one could easily take a half-day to do this hike. More like a mountain park than a wilderness area, this heavily used and well-maintained trail is a pleasurable and relaxing place to spend a few hours or an afternoon.

The trail follows the Roaring Fork River for a short distance before crossing it via a sturdy bridge with side rails. The river, wide and gentle through here, doesn't resemble its name. Shortly after the river crossing, the trail begins a gentle climb through dense aspen and fir. You'll come to a second stream crossing very soon. It is particularly important to observe good hiking practices in an area as heavily used as this one. Cutting switchbacks wears a trail very quickly that others will follow, creating a path for water flow and the potential for erosion. You'll notice as you hike that the Forest Service has placed downed timber and boulders in a number of locations where hikers have left the trail. It's inviting at times to rest on boulders or listen to the stream, but resist the temptation to forge a new trail through the delicate grasses and wildflowers.

The trail winds gently through the dense forest, reaching the lake in less than a mile. A trail of sorts continues all around the lake, situated in a small circle of treed slopes. The surrounding terrain is incredibly varied considering how small the lake is. This is a lover's lake, with numerous romantic and secluded hideaways; it's a child's lake, surrounded on two sides by a playground of boulders to play leapfrog on; it's a contemplative's lake, a fisherman's lake, a dedicated wildlife-watcher's lake. The hillside south of the lake was burned several years ago, but young trees are beginning to appear among the naked stalks that cover the hillside. Even the effects of the fire add to the beauty here—a stark reminder of the cycle of life.

If you're spending time in the Aspen area as a tourist or a wilderness explorer, or if you're just passing through and have only a few hours to spare, plan to visit this beautiful little lake.

The man who sat on the ground in his tipi meditating on life and its meaning, accepting the kinship of all creatures and acknowledging unity with the universe of things was infusing into his being the true essence of civilization. And when native man left off this form of development, his humanization was retarded in growth.

Chief Luther Standing Bear

Hikes in the Southern Area

These hikes are all easily reached via Cottonwood Pass Road (County Road 306), which extends east and west between Buena Vista and the Taylor Park Reservoir on Taylor River Road. The area is easy to get to; the lakes and streams are well stocked with cutthroat, brook, and rainbow trout; and most of the trails are well used and well maintained. From here you may climb 14,196-foot Mount Yale, hike the Colorado Trail, or begin an extended stay, backpacking, hiking, and fishing along the many interconnected trails.

Browns Pass Trail #1442

Destination: *Browns Pass and cabin*
Round-trip distance: *8 miles*
Starting elevation: *9,900 feet*
Maximum elevation: *12,020 feet*
Elevation gain: *2,120 feet*
Rating: *Moderate*
Time allowed: *9 hours*
Recommended use: *Day hike or extended backpack. Connects to Kroenke Lake Trail and Texas Creek Trail.*
Maps: *Gunnison National Forest; San Isabel National Forest; 7½' Mount Yale; Trails Illustrated Collegiate Peaks*

Trailhead Access

From the light at the intersection of U.S. Highway 24 and County Road 306 in Buena Vista, drive twelve miles west on CR306 (Cottonwood Pass Road) to the Denny Creek trailhead. Watch for the parking area and Denny Creek sign on the right (north) side of the road, about one mile past the Collegiate Peaks campground.

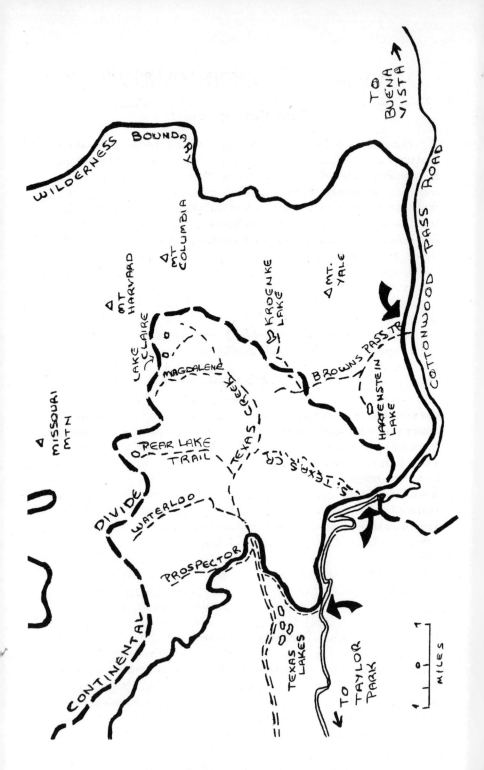

Collegiate Peaks Wilderness Area—Southern Portion

Trail Description

This trail is easily reached from Buena Vista in the summer and is a popular spot for hiking, fishing, and horseback riding. In the winter, the protected trail makes this an excellent area for cross-country skiing and showshoeing. However, Cottonwood Pass Road is closed during the winter months, so you will have to ski or hike the additional two miles from the winter closure gate to the trailhead.

Follow the trail description for Hartenstein Lake, on page 106. At mile 2, Hartenstein Lake Trail #1443 forks to the left and crosses North Fork Denny Creek. Stay to the east side of the creek for a short distance, following the main trail north. Within a few hundred yards the main path crosses the North Fork Denny Creek via a log. (The Trails Illustrated map shows the trail remaining on the east side of the stream, which is not as I found it.) The track winds through a variety of ecosystems—meadow, marsh, open valley, and, after a few switchbacks through a mixed conifer forest, climbs to tundra. Shortly after the trail breaks out of the timber, it crosses to the east of the creek and climbs gently above the willows. The view from Browns Pass is breathtaking, with the Three Apostles to the northwest and Mount Yale to the east. Browns cabin is located at timberline on the north side of the pass. This was originally a small settlement and shelter for pack trains and saddle riders moving into Taylor Park. Today it offers respite to hikers, skiers, and horseback riders and is maintained by the cooperative efforts of the Forest Service and volunteers. To reach the cabin, continue one-half mile down the north side of the pass. If you plan to stay awhile, bring a cabin "gift"—toilet paper, lantern fuel and mantles, candles and matches, canned food, books, and playing cards are all welcome items. Critter-proof containers are appreciated also.

Several possibilities exist from the pass. As a day hike this makes an excellent turn-around point. Those interested in extended backpacking in the area can continue north on the trail, dropping 1,300 feet to connect with Texas Creek Trail #416. The extensive trail system through there provides the possibility of backpacking for several days. To reach Texas Creek, follow the good trail northwest from the cabin. Within a few hundred yards the trail appears to fork. Ignore the left fork—it simply leads to additional campsites. Follow the right fork as it traverses the mountainside, passing through patches of forest and alongside boulder fields. At approximately one-half mile past the cabin the Texas Creek valley comes into view and remains visible for the remaining three-quarters

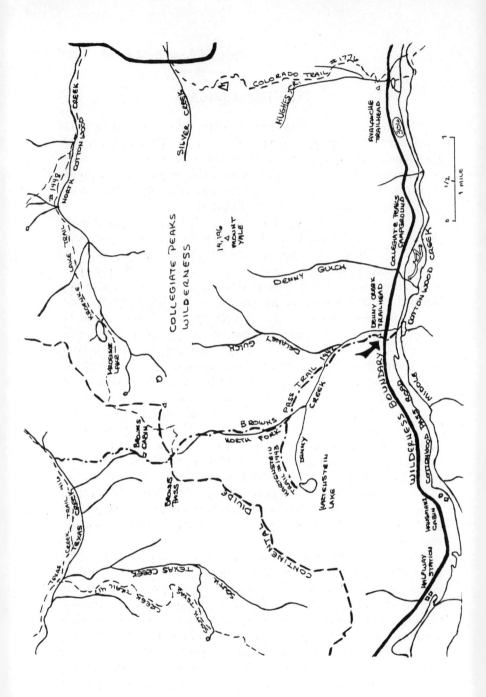

Browns Pass Trail #1442, Hartenstein Lake Trail #1443

Browns Pass viewed from the south along the trail.

of a mile to the well-marked intersection. From the intersection of the two trails, one may follow Texas Creek west to the unmaintained Pear Lake Trail #1461, then north out of the Texas Creek drainage and over the Continental Divide, ending on the South Fork Clear Creek Road. Another alternative after reaching Texas Creek is to head west along the Texas Creek Trail to connect with Timberline Trail #414. Follow this trail south to Cottonwood Pass Road or northwest for several miles, reentering the Wilderness Area on Red Mountain Creek Trail #543.1. From here it is possible to completely cross the Collegiate Peaks Wilderness Area via connecting trails, finally ending on Independence Pass Road. Or, you can explore any one or all of the numerous trails that connect with the Texas Creek Trail, returning back over Browns Pass to your original starting point at the Denny Creek trailhead.

A less ambitious extended backpacking trip might follow Kroenke Lake Trail #1448 east from Browns Pass, crossing the Continental Divide twice and ending at the North Cottonwood trailhead on County Road 365. A car shuttle would be required to get you back to your starting point.

Hills are always more beautiful than stone buildings, you know. Living in a city is an artificial existence. Lots of people hardly ever feel real soil under their feet, see plants grow except in flower pots, or get far enough beyond the street light to catch the enchantment of a night sky studded with stars. When people live far from the scenes of the Great Spirit's making, it's easy for them to forget his laws.

Tatanga Mani (Walking Buffalo)

Hartenstein Lake Trail #1443

(Refer to map on page 104.)

Destination: *Hartenstein Lake*
Round-trip distance: *5 miles*
Starting elevation: *9,900 feet*
Maximum elevation: *11,450 feet*
Elevation gain: *1,550 feet*
Rating: *Easy*
Time allowed: *4 hours*
Recommended use: *Day hike or overnight backpack. Excellent fishing. High-use area.*
Maps: *Gunnison National Forest; San Isabel National Forest; 7½' Mount Yale; Trails Illustrated Collegiate Peaks*

Trailhead Access

From the light in Buena Vista, drive twelve miles west on County Road 306 (Cottonwood Pass Road) to the Denny Creek trailhead. Watch for the parking area and Denny Creek sign on the right (north) side of the road, about one mile past the Collegiate Peaks campground.

Trail Description

This trail follows Browns Pass Trail #1442 (see page 101) for approximately two miles before forking to Hartenstein Lake. The trail terminates at the lake, making a delightful day's hike. Numerous campsites exist around the lake if you wish to spend the night. This hike is particularly beautiful in the fall, due to the dense aspen in the area. This scenic lake is well worth the effort required to reach it. Those who fish will have an opportunity to catch cutthroat and brook trout.

Begin hiking northwest along an old jeep road that has been narrowed and made into a trail. At approximately one-quarter mile you enter the Collegiate Peaks Wilderness Area. No mountain bikes or motorized vehicles are allowed beyond this point. The initial climb is fairly steep, passing through a dense aspen forest. The trail levels out after one-half mile, and the forest becomes mixed conifer and aspen. Denny Creek is on the right, but the trail soon moves away from the creek. Cross Denny Creek (10,500 feet) on a well-made three-log bridge. There appears to be a fork just before you reach the creek, but immediately after you cross the creek the trail meets itself and continues on to the northwest through a dense spruce forest.

Just past the trail sign to Delaney Gulch, at about one and one-half miles, the area opens up, affording spectacular views to the southwest. Mount Yale is visible to the northeast. The trail climbs steeply and the view continues to open up. Notice the beautiful rock outcroppings ahead as the trail approaches the creek again. The path forks at two miles, near these rock formations, crossing North Fork Denny Creek shortly after the fork. Take the left-hand fork—the right fork is the continuation of Browns Pass Trail #1442 and leads to Browns Pass and cabin.

The trail climbs sharply for a very short distance. However, it soon attains a wide ridge and levels out, offering impressive views of the Sawatch Range to the south. During the last one-quarter mile the trail once again enters heavy forest and willow. An easy mile from the trail junction you'll come to the crystal clear lake, surrounded by pine and willow. The trees quickly give way to the talus on the steep slopes curving down to the lake.

This lake will invite you to stay awhile, so be sure to take along a favorite pastime—journal, sketch pad, camera, or fishing gear. It's a perfect place to open up your creative self. It also presents opportunities for some interesting hiking and exploring on the talus slopes and encircling ridges.

The Delaney Gulch Trail is now the recommended route to Mount Yale (14,196 feet). Denny Gulch had previously been the standard route. However, due to the steepness and fragility of the Denny Gulch drainage, the Forest Service now requests that Delaney Gulch be used as the

14,196-foot Mount Yale is visible northeast of Hartenstein Lake.

principal route to climb Mount Yale. To reach the summit, follow the trail east up the steep drainage on Mount Yale's west side, then north to the northwest ridge for the final approach. Return by the same route.

There is nothing to do. Just be. No climbing mountains and sitting in caves. Abandon every attempt, don't strive, don't struggle, let go every support.

Nisargadatta Maharaj

South Texas Creek Trail #417

Destination: *Texas Creek Trail #416*
One-way distance: *4½ miles*
Starting elevation: *12,100 feet*
Maximum elevation: *12,400 feet*
Elevation gain: *300 feet*
Rating: *Moderate, expect some bushwhacking*
Time allowed: *5 hours*
Recommended use: *Backpack. Very faint trail at times, requiring use of map and compass. Connects to Texas Creek Trail.*
Maps: *Gunnison National Forest; 7½' Tincup; Trails Illustrated Collegiate Peaks*

Trailhead Access

From Gunnison, drive north eleven miles on Highway 135 to Almont. Turn right (east) and drive twenty-six miles along the Taylor River Road to Taylor Reservoir. Cottonwood Pass Road (County Road 306) begins on the east side of the reservoir, at the point where the Taylor River Road becomes gravel. Go east on the Cottonwood Pass Road for fourteen miles to the summit of Cottonwood Pass. Park in the parking area on the west side of the road.

To reach the trailhead from the east, from the light in Buena Vista at the intersection of U.S. Highway 24 and County Road 306, drive west twenty miles to the summit of the pass.

Cottonwood Pass Road was one of the many stage and wagon roads that crisscrossed this area during the early mining days to serve the stage centers in the Taylor River area. The stages waited for the trains passing through here, then took off with passengers and mail across the Divide to Buena Vista.

Trail Description

This hike begins just east of the Continental Divide and drops down into the Texas Creek drainage, where it connects with the Texas Creek

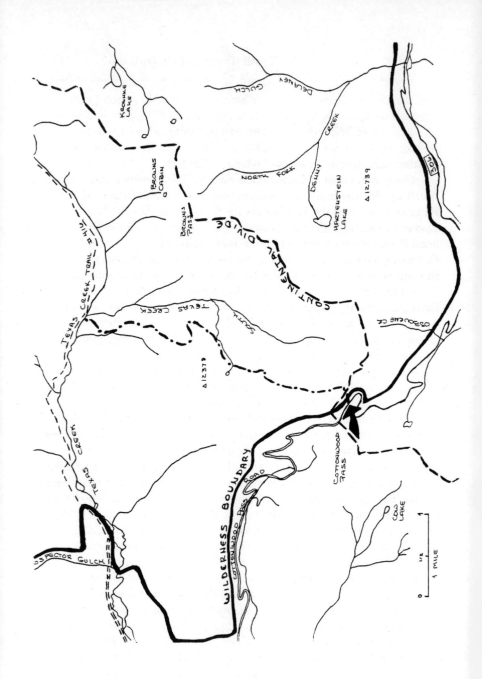

South Texas Creek Trail #417

Trail. The South Texas Creek Trail is an excellent starting point for an extended backpacking trip in the Texas Creek area. The hike begins at 12,200 feet and descends to 10,280, so if you were to hike it as a round-trip hike—from Cottonwood Pass Road to Texas Creek and return—the elevation gain would be approximately 1,920 feet.

The parking area at Cottonwood Pass may be crowded, but you'll quickly break away from the crowds as you head north and descend into the basin that forms the headwaters for South Texas Creek. The trail-head is well marked and begins about one-quarter mile east of Cotton-wood Pass. However, you may begin hiking almost directly across from the parking area, where you pick up the old Cottonwood Pass stage road. The remnants of this road parallel the present paved highway above and just to the north of the pass. From this vantage point you can see the old route down the valley to the east. Somewhere along here are the remains of Hangmans Camp. This isolated camp was located near a couple of mines just east of Cottonwood Pass. One can only guess at the reason for its name.

From the remains of this road, climb to the 12,200-foot pass, which rises northeast of Cottonwood Pass. Here you meet with the well-posted and cairned South Texas Creek Trail. Don't expect it to stay this way! Once you drop down into the basin, the trail becomes faint, the cairns have fallen, and porcupines have eaten off many of the marker posts.

The trail generally follows the western border of the basin, staying high above the dense willows. At a little less than one mile the trail begins a descent northeast, passing along the bottom edge of an extensive boulder field before entering a spruce forest. There are posts standing to mark the way through the trees, but you are well advised to carry a topo map and compass. The route is faint and easily lost.

A series of posts and cairns leads you through this initial forested region before crossing the second main drainage (at one and one-half miles and 11,680 feet). Stay well to the north of this creek as you begin to head east and work your way around the thick willows surrounding the creek. The trail is very difficult to find through here. Move into the edge of the forested area along the edge of the willows. The obvious trail finally emerges here—a well-trodden path through the fern-covered forest floor. The route passes close to a small lake tucked back among the trees. Continue following along the east side of this wide ridge.

One mile past the lake (approximately three miles along the trail) you break out of the dense woods into an open meadow. After the long, steep descent, this seems to be the intersection with the Texas Creek Trail.

The valley surrounding South Texas Creek slopes northward from the Continental Divide, meeting with the wide, long Texas Creek Valley.

A trail appears to go to the left and the right here. However, a turn to the right will take you into a confusing maze of cairn and faint forking trails. Apparently many hikers have lost the way here, setting up their own trail markers and creating numerous paths. Turn left instead, following the cairned trail to the north. Once out of the meadow and back in the forest the route becomes apparent again. The true intersection is obvious, because the Texas Creek Trail is well used. A shaky two-log "bridge" carries you across Texas Creek to begin your exploration of this valley. If you lose the route at any time, just keep heading north through dense spruce and fir to the unavoidable intersection with Texas Creek Trail #416. Off-trail hiking through here would be difficult, however, due to the steep slope and abundance of downed timber.

The South Texas Creek Trail leads to a halfway point along the Texas Creek valley. A number of different and easy car shuttles can be arranged. For example, you can go in here and hike out via Timberline Trail #414 or Browns Pass Trail, both of which are along the Cottonwood Pass Road.

The West of which I speak is but another name for the Wild: and what I have been preparing to say is, that in Wildness is the preservation of the World.

Henry David Thoreau
Reform Papers

Texas Creek Trail #416

Destination: *Lake Claire or Lake Rebecca*
Round-trip distance: *20 miles*
Starting elevation: *9,900 feet*
Maximum elevation: *12,300 feet*
Elevation gain: *2,400 feet*
Rating: *Moderate*
Time allowed: *2 to 3 days*
Recommended use: *Extended backpack. Connects to several other trails. Popular fishing area.*
Maps: *Gunnison National Forest; 7½' Taylor Park Reservoir; 7½' Winfield; 7½' Tincup; 7½' Mount Yale; Trails Illustrated Collegiate Peaks*

Trailhead Access

From the light at the intersection of U.S. Highway 24 and County Road 306 in Buena Vista, drive west twenty-six miles along CR306 (Cottonwood Pass Road). The trailhead is approximately five miles west of Cottonwood Pass. Look for the Timberline Trail sign on the north side of the road. You will follow this trail for two and one-half miles to its intersection with the Texas Creek Trail. Some parking is available slightly east of the trailhead and on the south side of the road. Additional space is available one-half mile farther east.

If approaching from the west, follow Highway 135 north from Gunnison to Almont for eleven miles. Turn right (east) on paved Taylor River

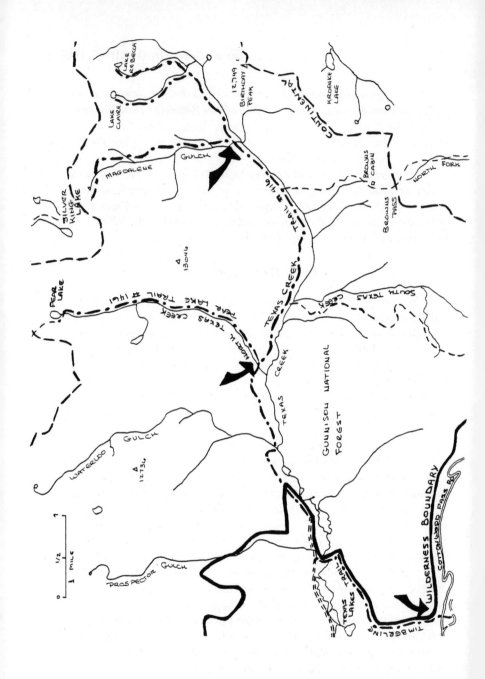

Texas Creek Trail #416, Pear Lake Trail #1461 (south), Magdalene Trail #542

Road (County Road 742). Follow this road as it winds its way generally northeast for twenty-six miles to the Taylor Park Reservoir. Here the pavement ceases and the road becomes gravel. Turn east on Cottonwood Pass Road and drive for eight miles to the beginning of Timberline Trail #414, on the north side of the road.

If you own a four-wheel-drive or high-clearance vehicle, the Texas Creek trailhead can be reached by continuing north on Taylor River Road one and one-half miles past Cottonwood Pass Road to Texas Creek Road (CR755). Drive east eight miles along this rough road to the Wilderness boundary and the beginning of the Texas Creek Trail.

Trail Description

Don't be put off by the distance or elevation gain on this hike if you are looking for a day hike or an easy backpack. This interesting valley has enough space and variety to satisfy all. The creek follows the wide valley floor, offering good fishing and numerous beautiful camping areas along the way. It's possible to backpack to within one mile of the lakes and still camp well below timberline, gaining just 1,700 feet in nine miles. Interesting side hikes ranging from easy to difficult can be made up the several gulches and creeks draining into Texas Creek from the north and south.

The hike description, distance, and elevation gain are given as if one begins hiking from Cottonwood Pass Road along the Timberline Trail. The Timberline Trail follows the western boundary of the Collegiate Peaks Wilderness Area for more than fifteen miles. This trail goes north and south from Cottonwood Pass Road. Heading north, it follows along the western boundary of the Collegiate Peaks Wilderness, providing access to the Wilderness at several points. South from CR306 it leaves the Collegiate Peaks boundary and continues into the Gunnison National Forest.

The well-used Timberline Trail is an easy trail to follow. The clear path heads north across level terrain and through a lodgepole pine forest. At one mile the trail turns northeast and begins traversing the mountainside and slowly losing elevation. Texas Lakes and the backdrop of the Continental Divide are visible to the north. The forest is mostly mixed conifer through here. After two miles you reach Texas Creek, having lost only 800 feet of elevation in this distance.

At the time of this writing the creek crossing was difficult. The heavy snows in the winter combined with heavy rain and fast melting in the spring caused the creek to change its course through here. A well-made

Texas Lakes and the Sawatch Range in the background from the Timberline Trail along the western border of the Wilderness Area.

bridge now crosses a dry streambed, while upstream a short distance a narrow log has been dropped across the "new" creek. It might be advisable to carry an extra pair of shoes, especially in early summer. Within a few hundred yards of the creek crossing the Timberline Trail intersects Texas Creek Road, which comes in from Taylor Park to the west. Turn east (right) and walk through open meadow for one mile to the Wilderness boundary. Ignore a right fork in the road at approximately one-half mile.

At the Wilderness boundary a sign directs you northwest along the Timberline Trail or east up the valley. Follow the route east, passing through lodgepole pine forest for a short distance. The Texas Creek Trail continues east, moving out to the edge of the forest and into the open meadow north of several extensive beaver ponds. Within three-quarters of a mile of the Wilderness boundary the road turns south for a few hundred yards, then back again to the east.

The sheer rock faces of the unnamed peaks east of North Texas Creek present an awesome view as you hike up Texas Creek. The sight of this steep barren rock accompanies you for a mile or so through the open valley. Here, you move away from the creek and begin a gentle hike through lodgepole pine again.

Two miles from the Wilderness boundary (five miles from the Timberline trailhead on CR306) you cross North Texas Creek. The faint track of Pear Lake Trail #1461 heads northeast from here, shortly after the easy creek crossing. This trail is not maintained or as heavily used as others, so it is difficult to find and follow. It does provide a way to cross the Continental Divide into the Lake Fork Clear Creek drainage and out to Rockdale on Clear Creek Road. However, I recommend it only to strong hikers familiar with off-trail hiking and the use of map and compass.

The intersection of Texas Creek Trail and South Texas Creek Trail #417 occurs at three miles past the Wilderness boundary (six miles from the Timberline trailhead). The South Texas Creek Trail leads steeply south four miles to 12,126-foot Cottonwood Pass.

Five miles past the Wilderness boundary you reach the intersection with Browns Pass Trail #1442. Many hikers prefer to begin their exploration of the Texas Creek area via this trail. One and one-quarter miles south along the Browns Pass Trail is Browns cabin, once used as a stop by miners passing from Texas Creek to the eastern slope.

If you are continuing on up the Texas Creek valley, follow the good trail northeast, staying to the left of the creek. The route continues through a wide and open valley, offering spectacular views all along the way. Another mile (six miles past the Wilderness boundary) brings you to the well-marked Magdalene Trail #542. This area makes an excellent base camp for backpackers. Good campsites exist here, tucked under the tall spruce at 11,100 feet—well below timberline. From this location one can continue on along the faint Texas Creek Trail, following cairn across the meadow and into the forest to fish, explore, or just enjoy the high alpine Lake Claire (12,160 feet) and Lake Rebecca (12,300 feet). Or, follow Magdalene Trail to the mining ruins and lake high in the basin just below the Continental Divide.

What lies behind us and what lies before us are tiny matters compared to what lies within us.

Ralph Waldo Emerson

Pear Lake Trail #1461, South

(Refer to map on page 114.)

Destination: *Pear Lake*
Round-trip distance: *6 miles (from Texas Creek)*
Starting elevation: *10,160 feet*
Maximum elevation: *12,085 feet*
Elevation gain: *1,925 feet*
Rating: *Difficult (route-finding, off-trail hiking)*
Time allowed: *2 to 3 days*
Recommended use: *Extended backpack. Can only be reached from Texas Creek Trail #416 or Pear Lake Trail #1462, North. Rugged off-trail hiking.*
Maps: *Gunnison National Forest; 7½' Winfield; 7½' Tincup; Trails Illustrated Collegiate Peaks*

Trailhead Access

This trail can be reached from its intersection with Texas Creek Trail #416, one mile east of the Wilderness border.

To reach the Texas Creek Trail, follow Highway 135 north from Gunnison to Almont for eleven miles. Turn right (east) on paved Taylor River Road (County Road 742). Follow this road as it winds its way generally northeast for twenty-six miles to the Taylor Park Reservoir. Here the pavement ceases and the road becomes gravel. Drive east on Cottonwood Pass Road for eight miles to the beginning of the Timberline Trail on the north side of the road. A large sign, visible from the west, marks the beginning of the trail. Some parking is available slightly east and on the south side of the road. Additional space is available one-half mile farther east.

To reach the trailhead from the east, drive twenty-six miles from the light in Buena Vista along County Road 306 (Cottonwood Pass Road). The trailhead is approximately five miles west of Cottonwood Pass.

Trail Description

Follow the trail description for Texas Creek Trail #416 (see page 113) to its intersection with the North Texas Creek Trail, two miles past the Wilderness boundary. Shortly after crossing North Texas Creek, begin looking to the north for signs of a faint trail. The track is difficult to discern but follows to the right of a dry, rocky riverbed—probably the old path of North Texas Creek. You won't know for sure if you are on the trail until you attain a sharp ridge and begin climbing steeply through aspen. This is one of the few stretches where the trail is obvious. Avoid the temptation to follow one of a number of left forks that lead down to the stream. The trail stays high above the stream for the first one-half mile. White water rushes past, 150 feet below the trail.

Keep a good sense of your whereabouts. The trail fades often, and you must move through dense undergrowth and over downed timber as you continue. Stay as close to the water as possible. Eventually a faint trail next to the stream will emerge, but even then the way will be difficult. The trail is unmaintained and fallen trees block your passage here and there.

At about three-quarters of a mile you reach a large boulder field on the right. On the way up the gulch I opted to leave the "trail" and climb to the top of the boulders. The lush foliage along the creek is beautiful but I was ready for a new hiking experience. I discovered on the return trip that an easier and more often used route exists around the base of the boulder field, near the creek. You also might have better luck keeping with the trail beyond the boulder field if you stay low. At the end of the boulder field the creek flows out of the ravine to the left, circling around and over large flat rocks and forming an unusual S-shaped waterfall. Climb up to the right of the waterfall. A good trail exists through the thick undergrowth beyond here.

At 11,000 feet, just past the end of a second boulder field, work your way into the forested area. A trail exists through here that will carry you most of the way up the valley. I found parts of it on the way up, and parts of it on the way down! The higher in the basin you climb, the thicker the willows become. At three miles you reach a high, broad expanse. From here until the final, steep climb to Pear Lake the route stays east of the stream. You may choose to stay in the willows close to the water or climb above them to the boulders on the right side of the basin.

Though it's a relatively short hike from the trailhead on Texas Creek to the lake, plan at least four to five hours to reach the lake. If you are

A view of Pear Lake from four hundred feet above, along the Continental Divide.

planning to include this portion of the Pear Lake Trail in an extended backpacking trip, it would be advisable to begin the hike on Clear Creek Road, the trailhead for the north section of Pear Lake Trail #1461. The route from the north is easy to follow all the way to the lake. That leaves this section, from Pear Lake south to Texas Creek, as the "downhill" portion. Read the trail description for the north section of Pear Lake Trail on page 43.

I rejoice that there are owls. Let them do the idiotic and maniacal hooting for men. It is a sound admirably suited to swamps and twilight woods which no day illustrates, suggesting a vast and undeveloped nature which men have not recognized.

Henry David Thoreau

Magdalene Trail #542

(Refer to map on page 114.)

Destination: *Magdalene Lake*
Round-trip distance: *5 miles (from Texas Creek)*
Starting elevation: *11,000 feet*
Maximum elevation: *12,470 feet*
Elevation gain: *1,470 feet*
Rating: *Easy*
Time allowed: *3 days*
Recommended use: *Extended backpack. Reached by hiking Texas Creek Trail (6 miles from Wilderness boundary).*
Maps: *Gunnison National Forest; 7½' Mount Harvard; Trails Illustrated Collegiate Peaks*

Trailhead Access

This trail can only be reached from its intersection with the Texas Creek Trail, six miles from the Wilderness boundary along Texas Creek. One may hike into the Texas Creek valley via South Texas Creek Trail #417 (page 109), Browns Pass Trail #1442 (page 101), or Texas Creek Trail #416 (page 113). Depending on the point of access, overall round-trip hiking distance will range from sixteen miles (if hiked from Browns Pass Trail) to twenty-seven miles (if hiked from the Timberline Trail to Texas Creek).

Trail Description

The Magdalene Trail hike description begins in a wide, open valley at the intersection of Texas Creek Trail #416 and Magdalene Trail, six miles east of the Wilderness boundary. The trail is marked with a sign and is well used. Large cairn mark the continuation of the Texas Creek Trail east up the valley to lakes Rebecca and Claire. Just past a creek crossing at 10,960 feet, turn north and leave the open meadow, beginning a steep climb through a dense spruce forest. Within one-quarter mile the

Don't let rainy weather stop you! The mist and clouds add their own mystical beauty to Magdalene Gulch.

route levels out for a short distance before it once again begins a steady climb, staying to the right of the creek. The trail follows to the right of the creek almost all the way to the lake. The path is obvious most of the way, only occasionally fading into marshy soil. The Forest Service has put up wooden signs to mark the way, but don't count on them to be there—porcupine seem to enjoy chewing on these signs.

At approximately one mile the forest begins to thin. Still, small patches of fairly tall spruce dot the valley, offering rest stops and protection from sun and rain. This "valley" is wide and beautiful—nearly one-half mile from side to side. The rolling terrain is sprinkled with willows and boulders, patches of windblown spruce, and, as you climb higher, patches of the characteristic high-altitude krummholz. The last mile of the hike is across open boulder-strewn tundra. The trail is faint through the tundra at times but is marked often with cairn and posts. It leads directly to the remnants of an extensive mining operation. An abandoned cabin offers protection from the weather. The lake, though fairly large, is hidden below the hillside to the north of the mine buildings.

Two smaller unnamed lakes dot the landscape one-half mile south of Lake Magdalene. The area immediately surrounding the lakes is marshy, but you can sit high above them on the hillside, protected by the cabin remains or the boulders, and enjoy the abundant wildflowers encircling the lakes.

Your hike needn't end here. Though no visible route exists, one may hike northwest up the steep slopes around Lake Magdalene to a low point on the Continental Divide, just to the left of a highly visible notch along the ridge. From this point at 13,100 feet you look down five hundred feet to Silver King Lake. If you are prepared for an extended backpack you may drop down into this basin and follow Pine Creek Trail #1459 eleven miles northeast to the trailhead on U.S. Highway 24. Be prepared for steep rock-scrambling on both sides of the Divide. This route is not recommended for beginning backpackers or those uncomfortable with steep slopes, loose rock, and high altitude.

Earth provides enough to satisfy every man's need, but not for every man's greed.

Mahatma Gandhi

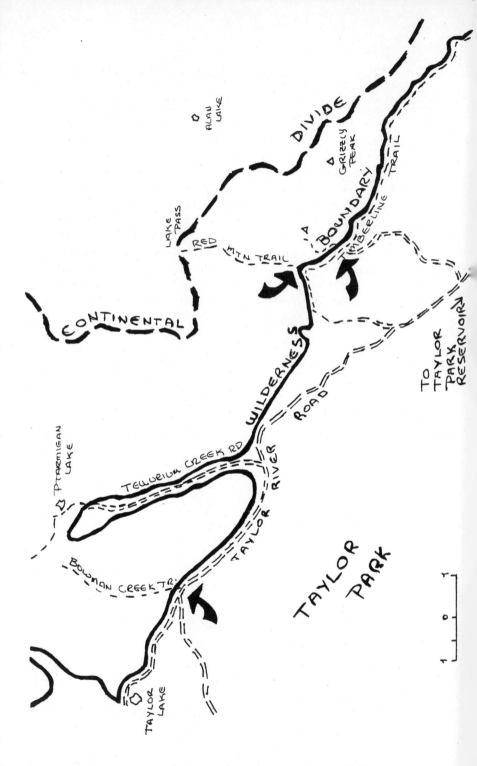

Collegiate Peaks Wilderness Area—Western Portion

Hikes in the Western Area

These hikes are all reached from Taylor River Road (County Road 742), which follows the Taylor River from Almont, eleven miles north of Gunnison, to its end three miles past the intersection with Taylor Pass Road. Taylor Park is worth the drive itself. The park is high and wide, and the Sawatch Range to the east rises quickly above timberline. At the southern end, access to the Wilderness Area requires a hike or drive along four-wheel-drive roads extending east from Taylor River Road. The central and northern portions are easily reached by standard passenger cars. Taylor River and Taylor Park Reservoir are popular for camping and fishing. Several campgrounds and camping areas dot the sixteen-mile stretch of road extending north from Taylor Park Reservoir.

Red Mountain Creek Trail #543.1

Destination: *Lake Pass*
Round-trip distance: *11 miles*
Starting elevation: *9,800 feet*
Maximum elevation: *12,080 feet*
Elevation gain: *2,280 feet*
Rating: *Difficult*
Time allowed: *8 to 9 hours*
Recommended use: *Day hike or extended backpack. Could be used to reach South Fork Lake Creek basin.*
Maps: *Gunnison National Forest; 7½' Pieplant; Trails Illustrated Crested Butte/Pearl Pass*

Trailhead Access

Follow Highway 135 north from Gunnison to Almont for eleven miles. Turn right (east) on paved Taylor River Road (County Road 742). Follow this road as it winds its way generally northeast for twenty-six miles

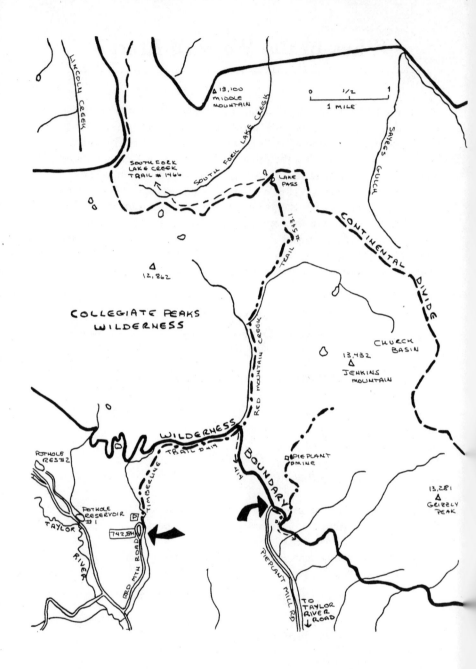

Red Mountain Creek Trail #543.1, Pieplant Trail

to the Taylor Park Reservoir. Cottonwood Pass Road intersects the Taylor River Road at the point where the pavement ceases and the road becomes gravel. Continue on the Taylor River Road for approximately seven miles to Red Mountain Road 742.8H. Here a sign marks the site of the historic town site of Red Mountain. It's unclear where the town was actually located. The early surveyor and explorer F. V. Hayden stated that the town was on the south fork of Lake Creek along Red Mountain Road. The town-site marker puts the dates of the town at 1873-1893. To reach Red Mountain Trail, follow Red Mountain Road one mile north through a pine forest. It ends in a wide loop. The trail begins on the east side of the loop. A number of campsites are available near the trailhead.

Trail Description

This hike has a wealth of variety—open meadows and beaver ponds; dense lodgepole pine forest; moist mixed conifer forest; high, willowed meadows; boulder fields; and a windswept pass above timberline. The well-maintained trail is obvious all the way.

The first two miles of this trail are along Timberline Trail #414, which follows just outside and parallels the Wilderness boundary. The hike is accompanied by the music of Red Mountain Creek most of the way. The trail begins a few hundred yards from the end of the road as you cross a log bridge that spans Red Mountain Creek. Immediately after crossing, sign in at the U.S. Forest Service sign-in box, just to the east of the stream. Another ten minutes brings you to a faded sign directing "Red Mountain 1." The trail forks right, climbing for a short distance and moving away from the water, then continuing through pine forest. At one mile you'll pass beaver ponds steaming in the early morning sun. The trail gradually begins to turn toward the east and once again picks up Red Mountain Creek, now on the north side of the trail.

At two miles you reach the Wilderness boundary and the intersection of Red Mountain Trail heading north and the Timberline Trail, which turns sharply back toward the southeast. Here Red Mountain Trail becomes distinctly fainter but still obvious. The hike continues through mixed pine and spruce. Just past the Wilderness boundary a collapsed log cabin looks out of frameless windows as you pass by.

Within a short distance you pass another set of beaver ponds. Algae tints the waters of these ponds bright green, and waist-high yellow flowers surround them. Like a Japanese garden, water flows here and there over low waterfalls. Another one-quarter mile brings you to the remains of an avalanche. The sight of one of these is always a little awe-inspiring. Seeing massive trees torn from the ground and scattered like pick-up-sticks, one can only imagine the power and sound of the slide that created this. Continue on through boulder fields and a mixed spruce and aspen forest. One more mile and the scenery changes again. Here you enter a beautiful open meadow in the narrow valley. For the first time, Lake Pass is visible ahead.

At four miles you encounter your first creek crossing since the start of the hike. On the map, this appears as a confluence of two creeks. When you are there, it's not so obvious. The trail literally becomes the creek, then disappears under thick willows. A distinct trail, a trail sign, and blazes on the trees let you know that you have found your way through the maze. The trail follows along on the west side of the "east fork." It begins a gentle climb through the dense forest now, passing an old log cabin on the right and crossing a drainage coming in from the northwest. The trail climbs more steeply as it switches back to the north. The steep ascent continues until almost tree line. I hiked through here with some effort, losing awareness of the surrounding forest and focusing attention on walking and breathing. It seemed almost suddenly that the terrain leveled out and the forest cleared. As I stepped into the open, the trees no longer blocked the view. Momentarily, it took my breath away. The panorama is spectacular —first the view of Lake Pass to the north, then southeast into Church Basin, and finally, far to the southwest, Taylor Park and the misty blue mountains beyond. May you, too, be gifted with clear skies on this hike.

In the basin just below the final ascent to the pass the trail crosses to the east side of the stream, now just a marshy seepage. Here the trail becomes faint. You'll be at the top within twenty or twenty-five minutes, so persevere for the final steep climb. If the weather is clear you'll get a view of Red Mountain just as you crest the pass—two miles northwest along the Continental Divide. Is this where the creek got its name? From the pass, you can continue west to meet South Fork Lake Creek Trail #1466. The trail is cairned but faint as it turns west and begins a traverse along the north side of the Divide, down into the South Fork Lake Creek basin. However, if you continue north be prepared for an extended hike with a car shuttle. The trailhead for the South Fork Lake Creek Trail is on Independence Pass Road.

And I've come to know the western standard of living as a planetary standard of dying.

Sam LaBudde

A view of Taylor Park Reservoir from Lake Pass.

Pieplant Trail

(Refer to map on page 126.)

Destination: *High basin*
Round-trip distance: *5 miles*
Starting elevation: *10,300 feet*
Maximum elevation: *12,000 feet*
Elevation gain: *1,700 feet*
Rating: *Easy, but steep*
Time allowed: *5 hours*
Recommended use: *Day hike. Interesting historical area. Spectacular views of Taylor Park.*
Maps: *Gunnison National Forest; 7½' Pieplant; Trails Illustrated Crested Butte/Pearl Pass*

Trailhead Access

Follow Highway 135 north from Gunnison to Almont for eleven miles. Turn right (east) on paved Taylor River Road (County Road 742). Follow this road as it winds its way generally northeast for twenty-six miles to the Taylor Park Reservoir. Cottonwood Pass Road intersects the Taylor River Road at the point where the pavement ceases and the road becomes gravel. Continue on the Taylor River Road for approximately four and one-half miles to the Pieplant Mill Road on the right (east). Follow this road north across open sagebrush meadow into a lodgepole pine forest for four miles to the historic town site of Pieplant. The hike begins north of town, just before the Wilderness boundary.

Trail Description

This hike begins its winding track up the mountainside just behind the Pieplant Mill. Since Pieplant is somewhat remote, standing four miles off the main road, it is one of the few mining towns in the valley that still has standing buildings. The town was named for the broad-leafed rhubarb plant growing wild along the creek flowing southwest from Jenkins

130

The Pieplant Trail begins directly behind the collapsing Pieplant Mill.

Mountain. Prospectors were happy to see the plant growing there, a reminder of home, and so named the town after this wonderful "pie plant." The plant does well in this area and can still be seen growing near the Taylor Park Trading Post.

The town of Pieplant is situated in a wide meadow three thousand feet below the summit of Jenkins Mountain. Park anywhere along the road in the open meadow, then begin hiking northeast from the main cluster of two or three buildings. A road heads along the front of the tall mill building. You may attain the trail by hiking along this road, exploring the mill site, then climbing up the steep hill to reach the trail behind the remains of the mill. However, the actual trail begins to the north of the mill, on the east edge of the meadow. Here a good trail can be seen heading north and south. Turn south and begin hiking along the road. It climbs steeply and within a few hundred yards rises above and behind the mill. The faint track of the Timberline Trail continues south from here as the main road switches back to the left. Continue on the main road. Within twenty minutes the road reaches the Wilderness boundary. No motorized vehicles may pass beyond this point. Hike around the Forest Service gate blocking the road and continue following the road as it ascends the western shoulder of Jenkins Mountain.

At approximately one mile the road turns sharply back to the north and curves around the extensive remains of the mine. The sound of water can be heard rushing to the right, but no creek is visible from here. Continue north along the road another one-quarter mile to a high meadow at 11,000 feet. The trail moves close to the creek, an unusually pretty stream snaking through the grass. This would make a beautiful campsite. The creek washes down from the ridge visible high above timberline to the north. The road now switches back to the left and again enters a mixed pine, fir, and spruce forest. Openings in the trees begin to offer beautiful views of Taylor Park.

Continue on another one-quarter mile to a point where the road switches back again, passing more collapsed remains of the mining operation. The road becomes steeper as it begins a steady northeast climb. It's difficult to imagine that vehicles at the turn of the century were able to ascend such a steep grade. In spite of the steepness, your reward comes each time you stop to rest and turn around, for each turn of the road offers a more spectacular view of the valley and beyond. Soon after leaving the remains of the mining operation, the first view to the northeast opens up. Far off on the horizon Cottonwood Pass Road climbs to the top of the pass. Beyond the pass Mount Yale towers like a pyramid to over 14,000 feet.

The last half-mile of this hike is very steep. It finally ends above timberline in a high rocky basin one thousand feet below Jenkins Mountain's west shoulder. The road traces around the rocky basin, stretching toward the tundra above the granite cliffs. Rock slides have wiped away the final section of the road.

The views from this basin are spectacular. The Sawatch Range stretches far to the south, and the Cochetopa Hills can be discerned in the hazy mist on the southern horizon. The steep cliffs surrounding the basin are dizzying as you look up. Hundreds of rock "fingers" stick out from the mountainside above.

Though the summit of 13,432-foot Jenkins Mountain cannot be seen from the basin, it can be climbed from here. Allow an additional two to three hours for the additional two-mile ascent and return. To climb from the basin, drop down and cross the boulder-strewn basin. Avoid the steep, loose rock surrounding the west and north sides of the basin and begin an ascent up the tundra to the northeast. The first few hundred feet are steep, but it levels out as you swing back around to the

The climb up Pieplant Trail is steep, but the views of Taylor Park and beyond become ever more breathtaking the higher one goes.

west and approach the low point on the saddle. From the 13,000-foot saddle, turn east for the final, gentle four hundred feet to the summit. Return by the same route. If your route-finding skills are good, you may wish to descend via Jenkins's gentle south shoulder. If you stay on the broad ridge, you will eventually cross the Timberline Trail, which you can easily follow back to Pieplant.

What we do or don't do as a species over the next 10 or 20 years is going to determine the fate of virtually every species on this planet.
Sam LaBudde

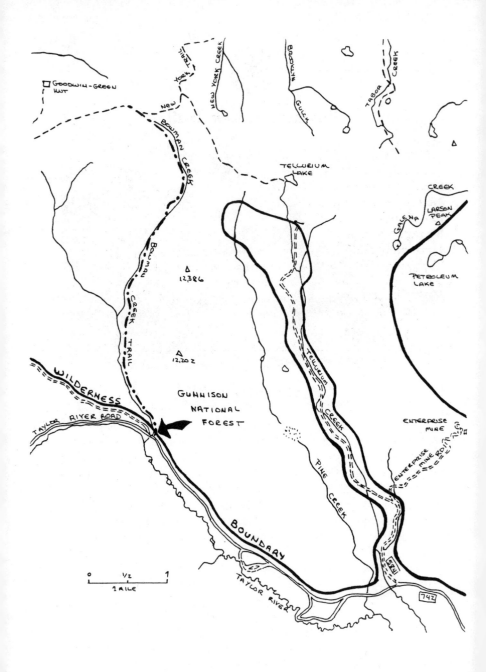

Bowman Creek Trail

Bowman Creek Trail

Destination: *12,240-foot pass at forest boundary*
Round-trip distance: *9 miles*
Starting elevation: *10,000 feet*
Maximum elevation: *12,240 feet*
Elevation gain: *2,240 feet*
Rating: *Moderate*
Time allowed: *8 hours*
Recommended use: *Day hike or backpack. Connects to New York Creek Trail for an extended backpack trip.*
Maps: *Gunnison National Forest; 7½' Italian Creek; 7½' New York Peak; Trails Illustrated Independence Pass; Trails Illustrated Crested Butte/Pearl Pass*

Trailhead Access

Drive eleven miles north from Gunnison, or seventeen miles south from Crested Butte, to Almont on Colorado Highway 135. Turn east on paved Taylor River Road (County Road 742). Follow this road as it winds its way generally northeast for twenty-six miles to the Taylor Park Reservoir. Cottonwood Pass Road intersects with the Taylor River Road at the point where the pavement ceases and the road becomes gravel. Continue on the Taylor River Road another fifteen and one-half miles, first north then northwest, to the historic Bowman town site marker on the right. The trail begins here as a rough jeep road but enters Wilderness in just a few hundred yards.

Trail Description

The drive through Taylor Park is worth the trip itself. The park is wide and high (10,000 feet) and follows along the eastern side of Taylor River. The majestic Sawatch Range rises quickly above the sage plain to over 12,000 feet.

Plan some time to explore the area along the drive. This was a boom area during the gold rush, and several well-preserved town sites still exist.

There are two U.S. Forest Service campgrounds along the road, Dorchester and Dinner Station. Dorchester was actually a booming mine camp in the early 1900s, with more than one thousand prospectors and miners in the area. Gold was discovered in the Italian Mountains west of Taylor Park in 1900, and Dorchester was dubbed the "mine camp of the new century." Unfortunately, snow covered the area much of the year, and getting the ore out was sometimes impossible. Nevertheless, some mines remained open all winter. Mining continued in the area through the early part of the century and finally closed down soon after the First World War.

The hike begins just west of the Bowman town-site marker. Begin hiking north up an old jeep road, staying just to the right of Bowman Creek. You will follow the creek all the way to its headwaters, so even though the trail becomes faint at times, the route is obvious. The first creek crossing occurs after about one mile; however, in June you may encounter two or three small drainages before this. Late in the season this stream may be quite shallow, but early in the summer you will need to make use of a small log that is dropped across the water just to the east of the trail. Shortly after the stream crossing the trail passes through a dense, tall patch of willows, but the route is easy to follow. For the first time you enter a mixed pine and spruce forest at 10,500 feet—until now the hike has been through open meadow and willows.

The track now becomes increasingly faint. Stay east of Bowman Creek and high above the willows. Have patience. The trail *will* reappear from time to time. As you continue on up the valley and enter another spruce forest, the trail becomes almost nonexistent. At approximately two miles the valley narrows and the trail begins to climb steeply up a forested hillside for one-quarter mile. At the crest of the climb you once again break out of forest into open meadow and dense willow. This is the headwaters for Bowman Creek—a high, wide meadow surrounded by a rocky hillside on the west that rolls around to the north, gradually becoming steep rock cliffs on the east.

The trail here is virtually absent. Begin watching for a place to cross to the west side of Bowman Creek. At this altitude the willows are short and sparse, presenting little barrier to your passage. Still, you will want to avoid the marshy water beneath them as much as possible. Bowman Creek is becoming less a well-defined creek and more a series of marshy ponds and streams. Work up to the low point on the surrounding ridge to the west, hiking generally northwest. From this pass you'll be able to view a high, wide plateau that rolls and curves to the west and north. What appears to be a good dirt road stretches to the west and its probable

The Bowman Creek Trail follows a wide and open valley for the first half of the hike. The destination is visible at the low point on the horizon.

intersection with Taylor Pass Road at the Wilderness boundary. The Goodwin-Green Hut, one of the huts in the Tenth Mountain Trail system, lies less than one mile to the northwest across level terrain.

If you are interested in an extended hike, you can travel directly north from the end of the basin (rather than climbing up to the northwest pass) and connect with New York Trail #2182. This good trail leads out to Lincoln Creek Road, which intersects Independence Pass Road. You may also wish to hike southeast, staying high above the basin, to Ptarmigan Lake. From there you can hike directly south one-half mile to the Wilderness boundary, then follow the Tellurium Creek Road six miles south to the Taylor River Road. This backpacking loop leaves you just five miles southwest of your original starting point.

The greatest delight which the fields and woods minister is the suggestion of an occult relation between man and the vegetable. I am not alone and unacknowledged. They nod to me and I to them.

Ralph Waldo Emerson

The Colorado Trail through the Collegiate Peaks Wilderness Area

The Colorado Trail extends 469 miles, from Denver to Durango. It snakes its way in and out of the Collegiate Peaks Wilderness Area for twenty-five miles along its eastern border. There are three places along this stretch where the trail can be reached by standard two-wheel-drive automobiles. The first eighteen-mile section of the trail begins at Clear Creek Road and enters the Wilderness Area two miles south of this point. It crosses Pine Creek Trail and Frenchman Creek Trail and ends at North Cottonwood Creek Road (County Road 365). The second, shorter section begins at North Cottonwood Creek and winds through the Wilderness for seven miles to Cottonwood Pass Road (County Road 306). This segment crosses the east shoulder of Mount Yale at 11,800 feet. A spur from Leadville to Gunnison is currently being constructed, and it will cross the Collegiate Peaks Wilderness via the Lake Ann Trail. From Lake Ann, the trail will climb to the Continental Divide, then drop down into Taylor Park.

The easy access and well-maintained trail through here make this portion of the Colorado Trail popular for day hikes and short backpacking trips. The connecting trails within the area offer the opportunity for numerous loop backpacking trips. Randy Jacobs's book, *The Colorado Trail,* is an invaluable aid to those interested in hiking longer sections of the trail. All proceeds from the sale of the book are donated to The Colorado Trail Foundation, a nonprofit organization dedicated to the ongoing construction and maintenance of the Colorado Trail.

Volunteers work on a spur of the Colorado Trail north of Lake Ann.

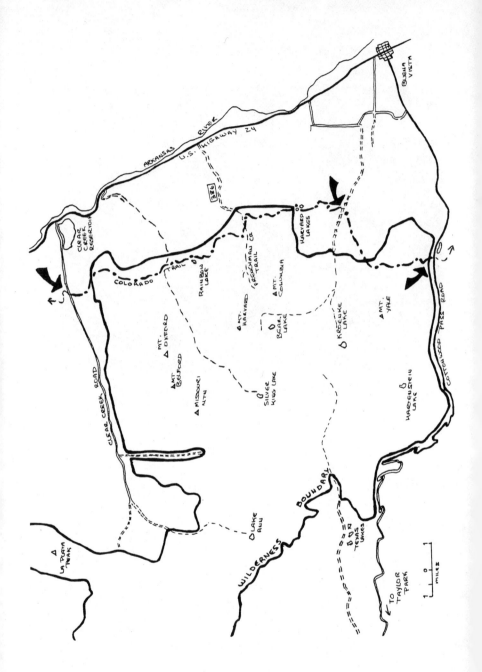

Colorado Trail #1776

Colorado Trail #1776 — Clear Creek to North Cottonwood Creek

Destination: *North Cottonwood Creek*
One-way distance: *18 miles*
Starting elevation: *9,000 feet*
Maximum elevation: *11,800 feet*
Elevation gain: *4,000 feet*
Rating: *Moderate*
Time allowed: *2 to 3 days*
Recommended use: *Day hike or backpack. Crosses Pine Creek Trail and Frenchman Creek Trail.*
Maps: *San Isabel National Forest; 7½' Granite; 7½' Harvard Lakes; 7½' Mount Harvard; 7½' Buena Vista West; Trails Illustrated Collegiate Peaks; Trails Illustrated Leadville/Fairplay*

Trailhead Access

This section of the Colorado Trail can be hiked just as easily from the north end as from the south end. It may also be accessed in the middle from the Pine Creek or Frenchman Creek trailheads. To reach the north end of this section of the trail, drive north from Buena Vista to Clear Creek Road (County Road 390), two miles south of Granite on U.S. Highway 24. Turn west and drive for three miles to the parking area on the north side of the road. The trail heads south from here.

To reach the southernmost end of this section, drive two and one-half miles west from Buena Vista on paved County Road 306 to County Road 361. Turn right (north) and drive two miles to CR365. Turn left (west) and follow this good gravel road approximately three and one-half miles to the trail. The road is rough and recommended for high-clearance vehicles, though standard two-wheel-drives can usually make it. Parking is limited at this end of the trail.

Trail Description

The trail heads south from the parking area through private property for the first half-mile. Lock the gate carefully behind you as you begin hiking south along the road past barns and outbuildings on your right to another gate within a few hundred yards. Continue on the road, still on private land, through a desert meadow dotted with potentilla and sage-brush. A true desert hillside rises above you to the north on the other side of Clear Creek Road, its barren expanse of sage testimony to the lack of water there.

The route heads east for a short distance. Just before a small knoll, it turns sharply to the south. Here you pass through the third and final gate and begin a gentle climb through a mixed pine, spruce, and aspen forest. The mixture of aspen and conifer makes this an excellent fall hike. The sweet aromas aroused by the late-summer rains, the rainbow of colors, and the wind through the drying aspen leaves all combine to please your senses. At approximately one mile the trail leaves the aspen forest and enters a lodgepole pine forest—eerily quiet after the noise of the aspen. The climb becomes steep as you work your way uphill to Columbia Gulch and the intersection with the faint remains of a road.

Continue the steep climb up Columbia Gulch, and at two and one-half miles you cross the Wilderness boundary. The path climbs steadily through aspen and pine for another two and one-half miles, finally achiev-ing Waverly Mountain's east ridge. Mount Harvard is visible to the south from this point.

The trail now drops quickly into the Pine Creek valley, losing 1,200 feet in elevation in one and one-half miles. Cross Pine Creek via a solid bridge. Pine Creek Trail #1459 heads east and west from here, following along Pine Creek. If you are interested in a loop backpack, you can hike west along Pine Creek for five miles to Missouri Basin and the Missouri Gulch Trail. Head north along the Missouri Gulch Trail for six miles to Vicksburg, five miles west of the Colorado Trail intersection with Clear Creek Road.

If you are continuing on the Colorado Trail, you may wish to rest in this beautiful valley awhile before beginning the ascent to the south. Leave Pine Creek and climb steeply along a switchback trail through mixed pine and spruce. Another one and one-half miles (eight miles from trailhead) and 1,200 feet brings you to a wide, flat knoll and high meadow. This would be a beautiful campsite but for the lack of water here. Rainbow Lake is hidden one-quarter mile to the west of the trail.

The route stays high (11,800 feet) for the next two miles, finally dropping down away from the beauty of the alpine flowers and wind-blown trees and moving to the side of Morrison Creek. Back under protec-tive timber now, the trail begins a descent to Frenchman Creek at mile 12.

The Colorado Trail is well marked as it winds through a dense section of lodgepole pine.

Soon after crossing the creek, the Colorado Trail intersects Frenchman Creek Trail #1457. The Frenchman Creek Trail leads west to a high bowl at the base of Mount Columbia and Mount Harvard. The well-used Colorado Trail continues south through spruce and pine, passing an old mine and faint signs of a mining road leading steeply down to the east.

The route continues a descent generally south to Three Elk Creek at mile 15. Here the trail leaves the Wilderness Area and passes between Upper and Lower Harvard lakes. These beautiful lakes offer numerous campsites along their shores, but camping is not recommended during the heavy-use months of July and August. Continue on through lodgepole pine and lupine, finally topping a ridge at seventeen and one-half miles. The trail drops down from here one-half mile to its end at North Cottonwood Creek. One-quarter mile west on North Cottonwood Road is the continuation of the Colorado Trail south.

It's not easy being green.

Kermit the Frog

Colorado Trail #1776 — North Cottonwood Creek to Middle Cottonwood Creek

(Refer to map on page 140.)

Destination: *Middle Cottonwood Creek*
One-way distance: *7 miles*
Starting elevation: *9,300 feet*
Maximum elevation: *11,880 feet*
Elevation gain: *2,580 feet*
Rating: *Moderate*
Time allowed: *9 hours*
Recommended use: *Day hike or overnight backpack. The high point is midway, providing the possibility for two shorter day hikes.*
Maps: *San Isabel National Forest; 7½' Mount Yale; 7½' Buena Vista West; Trails Illustrated Collegiate Peaks*

Trailhead Access

To reach the southern end of this section (Middle Cottonwood Creek), drive nine and one-half miles west from the stoplight in Buena Vista on paved Cottonwood Pass Road (CR306) to the Avalanche trailhead on the right (north) side of the road. There is ample parking here, though it may be crowded during the high-use months of July and August. Camping is available approximately four miles west, at the Collegiate Peaks Campground.

To reach the northern end on North Cottonwood Creek, drive two and one-half miles west from Buena Vista on Cottonwood Pass Road to County Road 361. Turn right (north) and drive two miles to CR365. Turn left (west) and follow this good gravel road approximately three and one-half miles to the trail. The road is rough and recommended for high-clearance vehicles, though standard two-wheel-drives can usually make it. Parking is limited at this end of the trail.

Trail Description

This segment of the Colorado Trail can be treated as two separate day hikes if hiked from either end to the high point along Mount Yale's east shoulder. It offers beautiful views of the peak from this point. It reaches the high point of 11,800 feet midway, gaining over 2,500 feet from either direction in three and one-half miles — a noticeable elevation gain, especially if done with a backpack. The view is spectacular, though, and this makes an excellent turnaround point for a day hike.

The trail description begins at the Avalanche trailhead on Cottonwood Pass Road (the southern end) and is given as if one were hiking the full seven miles to North Cottonwood Creek. Begin hiking northeast from the parking area. The trail follows along through a thicket of deciduous trees for a short distance before beginning a steep climb up a rocky hillside. The path enters a sparse pine and fir forest at 10,000 feet and continues its steep climb, switching back several times before finally leveling out at one and one-half miles.

Continue hiking north through a dense lodgepole pine forest. Good campsites exist through here close to Hughes Creek, which is fed by the melting snows from Mount Yale. At approximately two miles the trail leaves this level area and once again begins a steady climb, gradually becoming steeper as it approaches the top of Mount Yale's east shoulder. The trees are sparse at this elevation, allowing a magnificent view of 14,197-foot Mount Princeton to the south. Mount Princeton, though one of the Collegiate Peaks, stands to the west of U.S. Highway 24 and several miles south of the Collegiate Peaks Wilderness Area.

Begin a steep descent north from the saddle, entering into a mixed spruce and fir forest. At approximately four miles, cross to the north side of Silver Creek, passing several good campsites. One-half mile past the creek crossing (four and one-half miles from the Avalanche trailhead) the clear path moves away from the side of the creek and once again begins a steep descent north through a lodgepole pine forest. Continue for two more miles to the parking area along North Cottonwood Creek Road. If you are continuing north along the Colorado Trail, follow the road east for one-quarter mile. A trail sign on the north side of the road marks the continuation of the obvious trail north.

I like reality. It tastes of bread.

Jean Anouilh

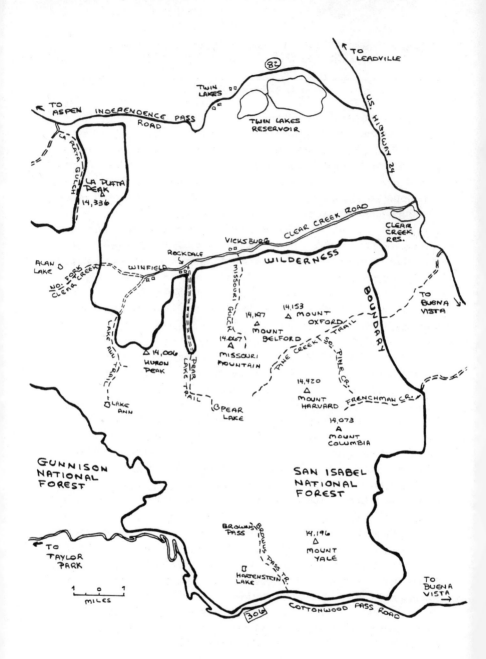

The Area Fourteeners

The Area Fourteeners

The Collegiate Peaks Wilderness Area contains eight of the state's fifty-four peaks above 14,000 feet. All of these peaks have nontechnical routes to their summits. Most can be hiked using no special equipment other than standard hiking gear—rain and wind gear, hiking boots, water, food, and first aid/emergency kit. Some, such as Mount Columbia, Missouri Mountain, and La Plata Peak, have some steep sections across loose rock and require the additional precaution of a hard hat. An ice axe (and knowledge of its use) should be carried throughout the summer on these peaks and others. Sudden thunderstorms at high altitude can turn even the easiest climb into a fatal experience. A quick descent down a steep snow-covered route may be required. If you are interested in increasing your knowledge of any aspect of hiking, the Colorado Mountain Club offers several low-cost programs to its members, covering every topic from weather and safety to equipment use. Many outdoor sports stores and community colleges also offer valuable classes in backpacking, mountain first aid, orienteering, rock climbing, and the use of ropes.

This guide is not intended to be a climbing guide to the high peaks in the area. However, since many of these peaks are reached from trails in the area, reference is made to their usual climbing routes. For more complete trail descriptions I recommend three guides that specifically address climbing these high peaks: *A Climbing Guide to Colorado's Fourteeners*, by Walter Borneman and Lyndon Lampert; *Guide to the Colorado Mountains*, by The Colorado Mountain Club with Robert Ormes; and *Colorado's Fourteeners*, by Gerry Roach. The helpful people at any of the Forest Service offices are also more than willing to inform you of the best current route.

In addition to the inherent personal danger in climbing above timberline, the areas around these popular peaks pose other special problems. Overuse of an area can destroy the very things that we seek to preserve in wilderness—solitude, pristine beauty, unspoiled landscape, and an opportunity to view wildlife. To avoid the destruction of these delicate ecosystems, we can help in several ways. First, when possible reduce crowding on these peaks by hiking during the week or on nonholiday weekends. Second, there are many other peaks that offer equal challenge; seek out and climb some of these less-visited peaks. Finally, as an alternative to the attitude of "conquest" inherent in the current Fourteener craze, learn the joy of hiking in wilderness with no destination or purpose greater than the experience of the moment and place itself.

For, to quote Robert Pirsig, author of *Zen and the Art of Motorcycle Maintenance*, "It's the sides of mountains which sustain life, not the top."

The following is a quick summary of these peaks and how to reach them. Refer to the trails mentioned for more complete descriptions.

There are two nontechnical approaches to **La Plata Peak** (14,336 feet). The first is from La Plata Trail (page 59), which follows La Plata Gulch. Drive west from U.S. Highway 24 along Independence Pass Road to South Fork Lake Creek Road. The second approach is from North Fork Clear Creek Trail #1463 (page 55), accessed by driving west from U.S. Highway 24 on Clear Creek Road to Winfield. Hike or drive along this four-wheel-drive road to the Wilderness boundary.

Missouri Mountain (14,067 feet) also has two approaches, equal in difficulty. The first is from Missouri Gulch Trail #1469 (page 37). Drive west from U.S. Highway 24 along Clear Creek Road to Vicksburg. The second approach is from Pear Lake Trail #1461 (page 43), on the west side of Missouri Mountain. To reach this trailhead, continue on Clear Creek Road past Vicksburg to Rockdale. Hike or four-wheel-drive south along the Cloyses Lake Road to the Wilderness boundary.

Mount Belford (14,197 feet) is climbed by hiking south along Missouri Gulch Trail #1469 (page 37), then heading east up its western slope. This gentle giant is one of the easiest peaks above 14,000 feet to climb. Tundra covers the slopes, and very little rock-scrambling is required. To reach the trailhead, drive west from U.S. Highway 24 on Clear Creek Road to Vicksburg.

Mount Columbia (14,073 feet) has one approach from the east and one from the northwest. The eastern approach is accessed via the Frenchman Creek Trail #1457 (page 23). Drive west on County Road 386 from Riverside, on U.S. Highway 24. The more difficult northwestern approach requires hiking into Horn Fork Basin, climbing Mount Harvard, then dropping down into the Frenchman Creek Basin and using the same basic approach as if one had hiked in from the east. To reach this trailhead, drive west on North Cottonwood Road 365 to the North Cottonwood trailhead and the beginning of Horn Fork Trail #1449 (page 15).

The approaches to **Mount Harvard** (14,067 feet) are essentially the same as the approaches to Mount Columbia. To reach the summit from Horn Fork Trail #1449, one hikes directly north from the end of Horn Fork Basin. To reach it from the east, hike northwest from Frenchman Creek Trail #1457 near the headwaters of Frenchman Creek. Both routes are long but can be completed in one day.

Mount Oxford (14,153 feet) is often climbed in conjunction with

Looking southeast to Huron Peak from Lake Ann.

Mount Belford. It's a long day when both are climbed but not much more difficult than that. The route between them is across a high alpine meadow with only a little bouldering required. Be sure to start early, however, because you will be above timberline and exposed to the weather for at least two hours. From U.S. Highway 24 drive west on Clear Creek Road to Vicksburg, then follow Missouri Gulch Trail #1469 (page 37) south.

Huron Peak (14,006 feet) may be climbed from the Lake Ann Trail #1462 (page 47). From U.S. Highway 24, drive west along Clear Creek Road to Winfield. Here an old mining road heads south along South Fork Clear Creek. This road becomes the Lake Ann Trail at the Wilderness boundary. The route to Huron breaks from the Lake Ann Trail within a few hundred yards of the Wilderness boundary.

The route to **Mount Yale** (14,196 feet) has recently been changed. The original route up Denny Gulch has been closed by the Forest Service. The steepness of the route and heavy use of it have created severe erosion. Approach Yale from Browns Pass Trail #1442 (page 101), which is reached by driving west from Buena Vista on Cottonwood Pass Road to the Denny Creek trailhead.

Appendix A
Suggested Backpacking Trips

The Collegiate Peaks Wilderness Area lends itself particularly well to extended backpacking trips. To follow are a few suggestions for trips of two or more days. Some require a long-distance car shuttle, some may be done with no shuttle or a very short one. Reference is occasionally made to Timberline Trail #414, though this trail is not described in this guide. The Timberline Trail follows the southwestern boundary of the Collegiate Peaks Wilderness Area. It extends north from Cottonwood Pass Road to Red Mountain Trail on the Taylor River Road. It is outside the Wilderness boundary and a popular trail for motorized bikes. For these reasons I have decided not to include it in this guide. However, it provides access to the Wilderness Area on that border. Red Mountain Trail can only be reached by hiking a portion of the Timberline Trail, and one of the easiest accesses to the Texas Creek Trail is via the Timberline Trail just south of Texas Lakes.

There are many other possibilities than those suggested here. For example, sometime in the near future the Colorado Trail will include a spur from Leadville to Gunnison. A major portion of this spur will cross the Collegiate Peaks Wilderness, with the Lake Ann Trail as a section of that route. You may wish to explore a route over the Continental Divide from Lake Ann to the Timberline Trail, then work your way back to the Clear Creek Road via the Pear Lake Trail.

I hope you will enjoy exploring the Collegiate Peaks Wilderness as much as I have. There are many untamed and untrailed areas there that have not been mentioned in this guide. I leave it to your imagination and heart to continue the exploration and enjoyment of this and other wild places.

Trails and Trailheads	Distance/ Elev. gain	Time	Rating	Shuttle required
South Texas Creek Trail (CR306) to Texas Creek Trail to Pear Lake Trail (Clear Creek Road)	15 miles 2,300 feet	3-4 days	Difficult (rugged off-trail hiking)	Yes
Browns Pass Trail (CR306) to Kroenke Lake Trail (U.S. Highway 24)	11 miles 2,400 feet	2-3 days	Easy	Yes
Browns Pass Trail (CR306) to Texas Creek Trail to Magdalene Trail to Pine Creek Trail (U.S. Highway 24)	20 miles 4,200 feet	4-5 days	Difficult (cross Divide at 13,200 feet; steep, off-trail)	Yes
Browns Pass Trail (CR306) to Texas Creek Trail to Timberline Trail (CR306)	13 miles 2,500 feet	3-4 days	Easy	Yes
Missouri Gulch Trail (Clear Creek Road) to Pine Creek Trail to South Pine Creek Trail to Frenchman Creek Trail to Colorado Trail (Clear Creek Road)	25 miles 7,500 feet	5-6 days	Moderate (long, but with good trail)	Yes
Kroenke Lake Trail (U.S. 24) to Browns Pass Trail to Texas Creek Trail to Timberline Trail (CR306)	16 miles 3,000 feet	3-4 days	Easy	Yes
Frenchman Creek Trail (U.S. 24) to South Pine Creek Trail to Colorado Trail to Frenchman Creek Trail (U.S. 24)	20 miles 3,200 feet	4-5 days	Moderate	No
New York Trail (CO82) to Bowman Creek Trail (Taylor River Road)	10 miles 2,200 feet	2-3 days	Moderate	Yes
New York Trail (CO82) to Brooklyn Gulch Trail (CO82)	10 miles 2,800 feet	2-3 days	Moderate	No
South Fork Lake Creek Trail (CO82) to Lincoln Creek Road (CO82)	15 miles 2,900 feet	3-4 days	Difficult (cross Divide at 12,900 feet)	Yes
Grizzly Lake Trail (CO82) to Graham Gulch Trail (CO82)	7 miles 2,000 feet	2-3 days	Difficult (high altitude, some off-trail)	Yes

Appendix B
Hike Summary Table

Trail	Round-trip distance	Elevation gain (ft)	Time (hrs)	Rate	Trailhead access	Connecting trails	Destination
Horn Fork Trail #1449	11	2,490	12	Difficult	U.S. 24	Kroenke Lake Trail #1448	Bear Lake; Mt. Harvard; Mt. Columbia
Kroenke Lake Trail #1448	8	1,640	7	Moderate	U.S. 24	Horn Fork Trail #1449 Browns Pass Trail #1442	Kroenke Lake
Frenchman Creek Trail #1457	12	3,240	1–2 days	Difficult	U.S. 24	S. Pine Creek Trail #1458; Colorado Trail #1776	Frenchman Creek Headwaters; Mt. Harvard; Mt. Columbia
South Pine Creek Trail #1458	8	1,400	6	Easy	U.S. 24	Frenchman Creek Trail #1457; Pine Creek Trail #1459	Pine Creek Trail #1459 (Little Johns Cabin)
Pine Creek Trail #1459	22	3,680	2–3 days	Difficult	U.S. 24	S. Pine Creek Trail #1458; Missouri Gulch Trail #1469; Colorado Trail #1776; Magdalene Trail #542	Silver King Lake; Little Johns Cabin; Bedrock Falls; Missouri Basin
Missouri Gulch Trail #1469	9	3,560	1–2 days	Difficult	Clear Creek Road	Pine Creek Trail #1459	Elkhead Pass; Missouri Mountain; Mt. Oxford; Mt. Belford
Pear Lake Trail #1461, North	13	2,100	1–2 days	Difficult	Clear Creek Road	Pear Lake Trail #1461, South	Pear Lake; Missouri Mountain; Iowa Peak; Emerald Peak

Trail	Round-trip distance	Elevation gain (ft)	Time (hrs)	Rate	Trailhead access	Connecting trails	Destination
Lake Ann Trail #1462	11	1,600	9	Moderate	Clear Creek Road	Silver Basin Trail; Three Apostles Trail #1462.2	Lake Ann
Silver Basin Trail	7	950	5	Easy	Clear Creek Road	Lake Ann Trail #1462	Silver Basin
North Fork Clear Creek Trail #1463	7	660	5	Easy	Clear Creek Road	None	North Fork Clear Creak; La Plata Peak
La Plata Trail	6	1,200	5	Easy	CO82	None	La Plata Gulch; La Plata Peak
S. Fork Lake Creek Trail #1466	15	2,100	1-2 days	Difficult	CO82	Red Mountain Creek Trail #543.1	South Fork Lake Creek
McNasser Gulch Trail	11	2,200	9-10	Difficult	CO82	None	McNasser Gulch
Mountain Boy Gulch Trail	3	660	2-3	Easy	CO82	None	Mountain Boy Park
Graham Gulch Trail #1478	7	2,080	9-10	Moderate	CO82	Grizzly Lake Trail #1990	12,600-foot pass
Grizzly Lake Trail #1990	7	1,955	7-8	Moderate	CO82	Graham Gulch Trail #1478	Grizzly Lake
Tabor Creek Trail #2185	6	2,100	5-6	Moderate	CO82	None	Tabor Lake
New York Trail #2182	8	2,140	9	Moderate	CO82	Brooklyn Gulch Trail; Bowman Creek Trail	New York Gulch
Brooklyn Gulch Trail	8	2,460	9	Moderate	CO82	New York Trail #2182	12,600-foot pass
Difficult Trail #2196	7	1,340	6	Easy	CO82	None	Difficult Creek
Weller Lake Trail	2	200	2	Easy	CO82	None	Weller Lake
Browns Pass Trail #1442	8	2,120	9	Moderate	Cottonwood Pass Road	Hartenstein Lake Trail #1443; Kroenke Lake Trail #1448	Browns Pass and Cabin
Hartenstein Lake Trail #1443	5	1,550	4	Easy	Cottonwood Pass Road	Browns Pass Trail #1442	Hartenstein Lake

Trail	Round-trip distance	Elevation gain (ft)	Time (hrs)	Rate	Trailhead access	Connecting trails	Destination
S. Texas Creek Trail #417	9	1,920	10	Moderate	Cottonwood Pass Road	Texas Creek Trail #416	Texas Creek Trail #416
Texas Creek Trail #416	20	2,400	2-3 days	Moderate	Cottonwood Pass Road	Magdalene Trail #542; Browns Pass Trail #1442; South Texas Creek Trail #417; Pear Lake Trail #1461,	Lake Claire; Lake Rebecca
Pear Lake Trail #1461, South	6	1,925	2-3 days	Difficult	Cottonwood Pass Road	Texas Creek Trail #416	Pear Lake
Magdalene Trail #542	5	1,470	3 days	Easy	Cottonwood Pass Road	Texas Creek Trail #416; Pine Creek Trail #1459	Magdalene Lake
Red Mountain Creek Trail #543.1	11	2,280	8-9	Difficult	Taylor River Road	South Fork Lake Creek Trail #1466	Lake Pass
Pieplant Trail	5	1,700	5	Easy	Taylor River Road	Timberline Trail	High basin
Bowman Creek Trail	9	2,240	8	Moderate	Taylor River Road	New York Trail #2182	12,240-foot pass
Colorado Trail #1776	18	4,000	2-3 days	Moderate	Clear Creek Road	Frenchman Creek Trail #1457; Pine Creek Trail #1459	North Cottonwood Creek
Colorado Trail #1776	7	2,580	9	Moderate	U.S. 24	None	Middle Cottonwood Creek

Further Reading

Borneman, Walter R., and Lyndon J. Lampert. 3d ed. *A Climbing Guide to Colorado's Fourteeners.* Boulder, Colo.: Pruett Publishing Company, 1994.

Colorado Mountain Club, and Robert M. Ormes. *Guide to the Colorado Mountains.* Denver: Colorado Mountain Club, 1992.

Eberhart, Philip. *Guide to the Colorado Ghost Towns and Mining Camps.* Athens, Ohio: Alan Swallow Books, 1969.

Jacobs, Randy. *Colorado Trail Official Guide Book.* N.p.: Colorado Trail Foundation, 1992.

Martin, Bob. *Hiking Trails of Central Colorado.* Boulder, Colo.: Pruett Publishing Company, 1989.

Rennicke, Jeff. *Colorado Mountain Ranges.* Helena and Billings, Mont.: Falcon Press Publishing Company, 1986.

Roach, Gerry. *Colorado's Fourteeners.* Golden, Colo.: Fulcrum Publishing, 1992.

Index